LIVING IN TUNE
WITH YOUR
HEART
THROUGH
RESONANCE REPATTERNING

BOOKS AND HOME STUDY COURSES
BY CHLOE FAITH WORDSWORTH

See ResonanceRepatterning.net for all Home Study Courses

The Resonance Repatterning® Series

- The Fundamentals of Resonance Repatterning
  Home Study Course: "The A–Z of muscle checking"

- Transforming Primary Patterns

- Transforming Unconscious Patterns

- Resonance Repatterning Process Guide

- Transforming Chakra Patterns
  Home Study Course: "Polarity Principles and Contacts"

- Transforming Five Element and Meridian Patterns

- Inner Cultivation through the Twelve Meridians
  Home Study Course available

- Principles of Relationship
  Home Study Course available

- A New Vision

- Energetics of Relationship
  Home Study Course available

Living in Tune Series

- Living in Tune with Your Light

- Living in Tune with Your Heart

- Living in Tune with Your Life

Resonance Repatterning® Books

- Quantum Change Made Easy

- Spiral Up! 127 Energizing Options to be your best right now
  Home Study: demonstration of all options by author

- Commitment to Life: A program for super health and vitality

LIVING IN TUNE WITH YOUR HEART
THROUGH
RESONANCE REPATTERNING

CHLOE FAITH WORDSWORTH
Founder and Developer of the Resonance Repatterning® System

RRI Publishing
A Division of the Resonance Repatterning Institute, LLC
ResonanceRepatterning.net
info@ResonanceRepatterning.net

The information in this book is intended for research and educational purposes
only. The author does not present any part of this work, directly or indirectly,
for the diagnosis or prescription of any disease or condition. People who use
the information in this book, or receive sessions from Resonance Repatterning
practitioners, take responsibility for consulting the health professional of their
choice regarding all matters pertaining to their physical and mental health.

Those who attend the Resonance Repatterning seminars use this material for
themselves, for friends and/or professionally, in accordance with the laws of
their country.

Cover photo: Rose Jones, UK – River Lea at sunrise. Used with permission.

Second Edition   2018
20 19 18   9 8 7 6 5 4 3 2 1   IV III II
ISBN 978-1-937710-26-2
Printed in USA

CONTENTS

WHAT LIVING IN TUNE WITH YOUR HEART IS ABOUT

LIVING IN TUNE WITH YOUR HEART is about what being human means. We know we are human beings, but being human is another issue.

Each of the next eight chapters gives us a different facet of the diamond of our humanity, pointing us in the extraordinary direction of being human.

The first three chapters – Seeing the Heart, Listening to the Heart and the Mature Heart – represent **the ideal**.

Chapters four, five and six – Disconnect from the Heart: trigger reactions and stress; Depression of the Heart; Triangles of the Heart – represent **the challenge** to living from the heart and being human.

Chapters seven and eight – Heart Abundance and the Joy-filled Heart – represent **transformation in action** and **the paradigm shift** in our thinking and approach to everyone, and our life, as we resonate with being human.

Most of us identify our heart with the organ in our chest, which we associate with love, compassion and kindness – particularly with love for those we are attached to.

However, in the East the higher octave of the heart organ, the true heart, is the eye center – an energy point between the eyebrows. This single eye is associated with the state of consciousness where we turn our mind inward and upward towards spiritual values, qualities and ideals. At this center of awareness and focus, love becomes universal: love for all beings, compassion for all, reverence for life – whether human, animal or plant.

When we resonate with spiritual values and qualities – embody them, live them in action – our thoughts, words, actions, how we relate with difficult people and stressful situations undergo a dramatic change. The transformation is practical. It is possible for all of us to integrate this new way of being human.

As we see in chapter 8, The Joy-filled Heart, there are nine principles lived by the Yequana, who have been called the happiest people on the earth. We too can embody these principles and transform ourselves and our life.

LIVING IN TUNE WITH YOUR HEART shares inspiring stories about some of the people who accessed this higher state of awareness, lived from this state of joy and benefitted all those who came into their company.

These people also raise the bar for us – encouraging us to live from this place of inner joy and love.

At the end of each chapter is a Resonance Repatterning process (mostly written for Resonance Repatterning practitioners), that makes the learning of each story practical in our lives. Even reading through these processes and doing the Energizing Option at the end will shift some of the resonance with unconscious patterns that act as an obstacle to loving ourself and others, and being human.

With or without the Resonance Repatterning processes, LIVING IN TUNE WITH YOUR HEART aims to serve each one of us who wants to:

- learn some fascinating information about issues related to the heart

- understand how we disconnect from our heart

- discover how to expand our heart's field of energy

- be introduced to new possibilities for hope offered by the Resonance Repatterning processes at the end of each chapter

- find out how we can shift our resonance with unconscious patterns from our past, and reconnect to our true nature of love and positivity once more

Chloe Faith Wordsworth
Scottsdale, AZ
September 2018

HOW DID THE RESONANCE REPATTERNING SYSTEM DEVELOP

I started developing Resonance Repatterning in 1989–1990. At that time I had spent six years in my private Acupuncture practice and twenty years studying numerous alternative systems in sound, color, movement, breath, energy and nutrition – always looking for the panacea for human ills and suffering.

In 1990 – when I finally understood that what we resonate with is what we experience and what we do not resonate with we do not experience – I discovered what I was looking for in terms of what creates positive change.

As a result of this understanding, I started creating the Resonance Repatterning system (originally called Holographic Repatterning). I began to integrate everything I had thought deeply about and learned from my private practice as a Five Element Acupuncturist, including everything I had learned from my studies and reading in Chakra energy systems, physics, psychology, brain research, vision and relationships.

However, I also wanted a method that others could learn and do on themselves, their friends, children and family members. The system needed to be profound, based on spiritual principles, and yet simple enough that others could easily learn it in order to

- identify the unconscious patterns we resonate with that cause our problems

- identify the life-giving patterns we **need** to resonate with in order to bring positive change when facing difficult life situations

- identify the Energizing Options from sound, color, movement, breath and energy contacts to change our resonance for the better.

The results were exactly what I had been looking for. Since 1990 thousands of people from around the world have learned Resonance Repatterning to make a positive difference in their own life and the lives of their families, friends and clients – and RR practitioners have experienced the same results that I have.

UNDERSTANDING MUSCLE CHECKING

New physics has confirmed that we are energy beings, existing in an ocean of pulsing vibrations or frequencies. Every thought is a frequency, every feeling is a frequency, and this body too is energy.

In the same way that radio frequencies are everywhere, vibrating in all directions, so our frequencies radiate everywhere.

To tune in to radio waves we need a radio receiver and a dial. Similarly, to tune in to our own and other's frequency waves, we also need a receiver and dial.

Our autonomic nervous system is that receiver and the on/off binary response of our muscles is the dial that tunes us in to our autonomic nervous system. The autonomic nervous system controls at least 90% of our unconscious functioning: heart beat, breathing, digestion, etc. – and all the 600 muscles of the body – which has made possible our survival over millions of years. Our autonomic nervous system knows what we need and what we do not need for our survival, health and mental-emotional well-being.

If we look carefully at our body, emotions and mind responses, we see that every aspect of ourselves is a feedback system: if we are sick, this gives us feedback that we are de-energized in some way. If we breathe rapidly, this gives us feedback, for example, that we are no longer calm. If we press on a muscle and it stays strong, this gives us feedback that nerve impulses are flowing to that muscle and the muscle is energized. If we press on a muscle and it weakens, this gives feedback that nerve impulses are compromised and the muscle is de-energized.

All feedback responses are mediated through the autonomic nervous system and the reflex responses of our muscles.

When a Resonance Repatterning Practitioner uses the on/off (strong/relaxed) binary response of a muscle, he/she is dialing in to the autonomic nervous system. The on/off muscle response, correctly used, provides feedback from the autonomic nervous system on what energizes us and what does not energize us.

Using the feedback response of our reflex muscles, associated with the autonomic nervous system (ANS), a practitioner is able to discover which energizing options are most beneficial at any moment in time: yes this energizes (strong muscle response); no this de-energizes (weak muscle response).

In India and China, doctors of Acupuncture and Ayurveda read the pulses to give equally important feedback on exactly what is going on in the body, emotions and mind and what a client may need to support health and wholeness.

In Japan some practitioners use the breath as feedback from the autonomic nervous system.

Some Chiropractors use the length of the legs to give feedback from the ANS.

In the West, kinesiology – or the binary on/off muscle response – is used to access our physical, emotional and mental field of frequencies.

Muscle checking takes training and each school and alternative healing method has its own theory and practice concerning this tool.

Resonance Repatterning practitioners, trained in Resonance Repatterning, understand the cues – (**mcs**) and *[**cr**] to be found in the Repatterning processes. (**mcs**), meaning muscle check yourself, refers to feedback on what each person needs in the Repatterning, and *[**cr**], meaning check the resonance, provides feedback on the positive and negative statements or actions we resonate with.

The *(off/umb off)* cue refers to the fact that at first we **do not** resonate with the positive statements and the *(on/umb on)* cue identifies that at first we **do** resonate with the negative. Once we complete the Energizing Option at the end of the Repatterning process, we are able to confirm that the resonance patterns identified in the session have changed.

HOW TO BENEFIT FROM THE REPATTERNING PROCESSES
IF YOU HAVE NOT STUDIED RESONANCE REPATTERNING

For those who have not studied Resonance Repatterning, there are various options in terms of the nine Repatternings at the end of each chapter:

- You can read the Repatterning and answer the questions, which may bring you a deeper understanding of yourself, your problems and how to move in the direction of self-mastery and bringing more love and harmony to your relationships and life.

- If you have not studied muscle checking, wherever it says (**mcs**) you will make an educated guess or intuitive choice as to which statement you need.

- If you feel you need a particular Repatterning, you are welcome to contact a Resonance Repatterning practitioner and have a session in person, over the phone or online. Working with a trained professional always brings results that you cannot get simply by reading.

- You can also take a few RR seminars and learn the muscle checking process so you can begin to apply parts of the Repatterning on yourself.

- The Repatterning processes in this book, powerful as they are, are only one major facet of the complete system. To give Resonance Repatterning sessions to family members, friends or professionally, training – in-person or online – is needed.

1. SEEING THE HEART

We who lived in concentration camps can remember the
men who walked through the huts comforting others, giving
away their last piece of bread. They may have been few in
number, but they offer sufficient proof that everything can
be taken away from a man but one thing: the last of the
human freedoms – to choose one's attitude in any given set
of circumstances, to choose one's way. The way in which man
accepts his fate and all the suffering it entails, the way in which
he takes up his cross, gives him ample opportunity – even in
the most difficult circumstances – to add a deeper meaning to
his life.

Victor Frankl, *Man's Search for Meaning*

A smile is all I have to give.

The story of the Smiling Man
Marci Shimoff, *Happy for No Reason*

Gandhi said if a single person achieves the highest kind of love,
"it will be sufficient to neutralize the hate of millions."

Allan A. Hunter, *Courage in Both Hands*

In Chinese medicine the sages of old understood that the heart – known as
the Supreme Controller or Emperor – is the home of the shen: the spirit of
unconditional love and compassion for all. Not just those close to us.

When the shen or spirit of love in our heart connects to the spirit of love in
another's heart, this, they say, is when the most powerful healing occurs. This
peak moment of loving connection is always life-changing.

THE OLD MAN AND THE DRUNKARD

In his book, *Safe and Alive*, Terry Dobson tells of an experience he had in Japan where he had been studying aikido for three years.

One afternoon while Terry was sitting on a train, a drunkard got on. Yelling obscenities, screaming, his hair encrusted with filth, he tried to hit a young woman who was holding her baby. She fell unharmed into the lap of an elderly couple.

Terry immediately stood up, ready to fight. Then he remembered the words of his aikido teacher: *Whoever has the mind to fight has broken his connection with the universe. If you try to dominate other people, you are already defeated.*

At the same time Terry also knew that he wanted to save the innocent and destroy the guilty. The drunkard now focused his rage on the young foreigner standing before him and punched a metal pole for emphasis. Terry gave the drunkard a look of disgust and prepared himself for what was to come.

Then something interesting happened. Before the drunkard could move towards Terry, someone shouted "Hey!" – loudly but with a strangely joyous, lilting quality in his voice. Both Terry and the drunkard turned to see an old man who was beaming with delight, gazing up at the drunkard. The old man beckoned to the drunk man and said, "C'mere and talk with me."

The drunkard now stood threateningly in front of the old man, who continued to smile at him. "Wha'cha been drinking?" the old man asked, his eyes fearless and sparkling with interest. "Sake," the drunkard bellowed. The old man began to tell the drunkard that he and his wife would take their sake into the garden and watch the sun go down; and they liked to see how their persimmon tree was doing. His great-grandfather had planted that persimmon and they didn't know if it would survive the frosts.

The drunkard was softening: "Yeah, I love persimmons too."
And the old man said, "And you have a wonderful wife?" No:
no wife, no home, no job, no money and nowhere to go. The old
man beckoned to him, "Sit down and tell me about it." Within
minutes the drunkard's head was on the old man's lap. The old
man softly stroked the drunkard's matted head, his face filled with
compassion. Tears rolled down the drunkard's cheeks as he shared
his story of despair.

If doing the Repatterning, return to {A a} p.17

Out of sync light waves

Light waves that are disorganized bump into each other. This is known as
destructive interference. Light waves that are out of sync with each other weaken
each other and may even cancel each other out.

Our own disorganized light waves diminish the power of our heart's light and
love. A 60-watt light bulb doesn't radiate much light, or reach very far. When our
light waves are out of sync, we lose our awareness of the creative principle of love
within, our light is diminished and it doesn't radiate very far.

In-sync light waves

When the light waves of our heart are organized, then, like a laser, our light waves
are penetrating and have huge power.

It takes only a small wattage to create the power of a laser beam, whereas it takes a
lot of energy to produce the light waves of an ordinary 60-watt light bulb.

Doc Childre, founder of HeartMath Institute, comments that the shift from non-
coherence to coherence has dramatic effects. For instance, if the non-coherent
light waves of a 60-watt light bulb could be made as coherent as a laser, they
would have the power to bore a hole through the sun!

This is the power of the heart's love.

In tune with the creative principle of love
With very little effort or energy expenditure, the old man was like a laser beam of light for all those on the train – and even for us, who read his story.

He understood the creative principle of unconditional love. His frequencies were attuned to love, and his actions reflected this attunement.

The young man, Terry, in spite of his aikido training, wasn't yet aware of this creative principle of the heart in action.

The power of our light
Physicists believe that all matter is composed of trapped light. Mystics in the East explain that our pulsing field of energy is of sound and light. This means we produce millions of wave frequencies – an immense orchestra of sound and light.

We are energy beings. Yet how many of us feel like 60 watt light bulbs?

Neutralizing hate through the shen of the heart
In the story of the old man and the drunkard, what we see is that because the young man had non-coherent wave frequencies, he couldn't radiate his light and calm the drunkard. Instead of having a transformative effect on him, he only incensed the drunkard further.

The drunkard's wave frequencies were even more disorganized and non-coherent. The result of the wave frequencies of these two men meeting each other could only lead to yet more destructive interference – canceling out the light of their heart's love.

And then there was the old man. His coherent, ordered frequencies were reflected in his joy, his understanding, his ability to calm the drunkard through his empathy and compassion. His was the power of the laser – the primal sound-light energy within – the heart's love that heals the hearts of all.

The Emperor of the Heart commands without commanding, acts without acting, heals with a joyful "Hey... C'mere and talk with me!"

In that state the Heart is like an Emperor who rules through love and compassion. The Heart radiates the divine spirit of love through the light of the eyes.

This shen spirit of love – our true nature – is within each of us, no matter what we have done or how we have lived.

ONE SPOT OF LIGHT

Dr. Emoto's pictures show how water crystals change their shape according to the thought or words written on the glass container.

Once Dr. Emoto wrote the word "Hitler" on the glass container. The crystal picture that resulted was dark and chaotic.

But when Dr. Emoto magnified the picture over and over again, he was finally able to see one spot of light.

This point of light in all of us is the unchanging power of the Divine. It is the primal light and sound of our essence, the creative principle of unconditional love. It is the purest and most coherent energy there is. And it is the heart of who we are, which can never be erased.

If doing the Repatterning, return to {A c} p.17

If doing the Repatterning, return to {A c} p.17

Experiencing love

The difference between Hitler and the wise one – the sage – is the level of awareness and realization of this creative principle of unconditional love.

Even in the smallest of actions, we can either connect to or disconnect from our heart's love. We can either increase or decrease our own spot of light and love.

Hugging on the left side or the right side

Every thought, word and action either gives us energy and expands our heart's love or depletes us of energy and decreases our capacity to experience our heart's love.

For instance, you can ask a Resonance Repatterning practitioner to do the following experiment with you. First of all give each other a hug the conventional way – both of you connecting on the right side of the body. Then have the practitioner check your muscle strength for whether this expands your heart's energy and connects you to the heart/light within. Your muscles will weaken because this kind of hug depletes your heart energy and disorders your frequencies.

Now both of you hug on the **left** side of the body – heart to heart. Once again have the practitioner check the strength of your muscles. This time your muscles stay strong, illustrating that a heart-to-heart left-sided hug energizes both people, creating coherent, ordered frequencies in your heart/light energy.

It is the same with every action, word and thought. Even seemingly insignificant non-truths weaken our energy field and diminish our capacity to experience love. A weakened, non-coherent energy field enables further non-truths. And the downward spiral keeps going until we have corruption, a loss of spiritual values, anger, conflict, violence and a world at war.

Inner cultivation

So how can we become laser beams of coherent light and open our heart to unconditional love?

This involves a life-long practice of what the ancient Taoists called inner cultivation.

Ultimately inner cultivation of our true nature only comes about through grace. We become receptive to grace through our spiritual practice of meditation and contemplation under the guidance of a teacher who has experienced and lives the creative principle of love. Grace comes **from the inside** and involves the inner work of raising our consciousness by stilling our mind. Only then can we experience the heart's love within.

Systems like Resonance Repatterning support our growing awareness of the heart's light and love within, and the possibility of creating coherence in our daily lives **from the outside**. This is the practical **outer** work of putting in the effort to become good human beings by resonating with what is positive and life-giving and accepting all experiences – the so-called bad along with the so-called good – as a divine gift.

Returning to our natural resonant vibration
To be truly coherent we need a way to support all our frequencies to return to the vibration they most naturally vibrate at.

Any negative in our life is a wake-up call that lets us know we have lost our natural resonant vibration – that it is time to come back on track with our true nature, with our heart.

There is nothing but the positive
All positive qualities are the outcome of natural resonance and coherence in our field. It is only when we are out of tune with the positive, with our natural resonance, that we experience the shadow side – what appears to be negative.

Negativity is an illusion. Negativity is simply a lack of awareness or realization of the heart's love within.

As we re-establish our natural resonance, we begin to vibrate in tune with the primal sound and light within, and we automatically experience the positive in whatever circumstances we find ourselves in.

When we vibrate according to our heart's natural resonance, we are in tune with the harmony in all others. This is how the old man transformed the drunkard's violence, and this is how each one of us has the potential to transform any disaster into an opportunity for transcendence.

A SMILE IS ENOUGH

When a teenager called Happy had just completed high school, she decided to go to Bangladesh.

She arrived to discover that the monsoon season was at its height with constant and heavy rains. In addition, there was widespread famine and people were dying all over the country.

Happy decided to go by bus to the more remote villages. At one point the road had been washed away and the bus was forced to stop on an island of higher ground the size of a football field.

Soon hundreds of people from a nearby flooded village were making their way to this island of higher ground. The people were in rags and to her horror they were dying of dysentery and starvation. There was no food, and no water to drink.

Feeling helpless, she began to cry. Then she saw a man standing outside her bus window gazing up at her. Like everyone else he was skinny and barefoot, but unlike them he was smiling.

Still upset, Happy snapped at him, "How can you smile in such a situation?" The man answered in perfect Queen's English, "A smile is all I have to give, madam."

He told her to come with him, and they spent the next ten hours in the rain, walking through the field, singing to each person who was dying. This man – Smiling Man, she called him – eased the suffering of hundreds of people with his beautiful Muslim chants, his love and joy.

She ends her story, "The Smiling Man showed me that giving love to others isn't complicated or difficult. I know firsthand that when a smile is all you have to give, it can be enough."

If doing the Repatterning, return to {G} p.23

Giving what we have

Giving what we have depends on regaining our natural resonance – the frequency of the heart.

In India, the higher octave of what we call our heart is the brow center – where we connect to the reality of the inner light and sound within ourselves.

In the Christian tradition the brow center is called the single eye. "If thine eye be single, thy whole body shall be filled with light."

Only when we raise our consciousness to this true heart center do the frequencies of our mind become ordered and harmonized – full of light.

As the chatter of the mind becomes still, we experience the higher qualities of mind and spirit: deep inner relaxation, peace, joy, and love for all. Little by little we are transformed from low-wattage light bulbs to powerful laser beams of light. Then, like the sage, the Smiling man, whatever we give, it is enough.

FURTHER READING

Doc Childre. *The HeartMath Solution.*

Terry Dobson. *Safe and Alive.*

Marci Shimoff. *Happy for No Reason.*

1. SEEING THE HEART REPATTERNING

A. Identify the heart's intention

Do {a–e} in sequence.

a. Read the story of the old man and the drunkard *p.8*

Ask, "What does this story mean for you?" *[cr] with "I (*name the positive meaning*)" *(will be off/umb off).*

b. The heart you are closed to

Ask, "Whose heart are you closed to? What keeps your heart closed to (*name the person/people*)?"

*[cr] with "My heart is closed to (*name the person/people*) because (*name the reason*)" *(will be on/umb on because at this time client resonates with a closed heart in this situation).*

c. Read or tell the story of one spot of light *p.11*

Ask, "What does this story mean for you?" *[cr] with "I am receptive to my heart's compassion and see (*name the positive meaning*)" *(will be off/ umb off).*

d. What does your heart want?

Ask, "What does your heart most want in relation to (*name person*) and in your life?

*[cr] with "I (*name what the heart wants – omitting 'want'*)" *(will be off/ umb off because client does not yet resonate with the heart's intention).*

e. Identify the connection needed

Write down the following statement: "I am an inseparable part of the ocean of unconditional love, as is (*name the person your heart is closed to*). I radiate this gift of love to (*name person*) and to all beings."

*[cr] *(will be off/umb off because at this time client's frequencies are out of sync with their natural resonance).*

B. **Identify the non-coherent qualities in the Heart Official that close the heart's awareness to the light of unconditional love** (**mcs**) {1–15} for the primary quality involved. *You may need to insert the name of the person/people involved from {A b}.* *[**cr**] *(will be on/umb on).*

   1. I am over-controlling.
   2. I feel out of control.
   3. I am driven to try and connect with everyone, but I feel alone and without a real friend.
   4. (I can't relax into heart silence • I keep talking excessively).
   5. My life swings between control and chaos.
   6. I swing between dominance and submission in my relationships.
   7. I communicate from my head without heart warmth.
   8. My mind controls my life, rather than my intuitive knowing and heart's love leading my life.
   9. I am uncomfortable making loving eye contact with (*name person/ people*).
   10. I am unable to receive the love that others give me.
   11. I am constantly searching for joy, happiness and pleasure in the world rather than from within myself.
   12. I close my heart as a way to avoid pain and disappointment.
   13. I often/sometimes feel out of control emotionally and mentally.
   14. I am taken in by appearances.
   15. I am unable to see and connect to (a person's • *name person*)'s inner nature.

C. **Identify what closes the heart's awareness to the creative principle of unconditional love?**
   Do {a–d} in sequence.
   a. **Identify the fear involved**
      Ask, "What or who are you afraid of?"
      *[**cr**] with "I am afraid that (*name the fear*), even though this fear disconnects me from my heart's shen of unconditional love" *(will be on/umb on because client resonates with disconnecting from the heart through fear).*

b. **(mcs) Any of the following fears are needed?**
Write down the following: "I am afraid of (betrayal • abandonment• humiliation • rejection • failure) even though this fear disconnects me from my heart's shen of unconditional love."
*[cr] *(will be on/umb on because client resonates with this fear, which blocks the opening of the heart to love).*

c. **Identify the anger involved**
Ask, "What makes you angry?"
*[cr] with "I get angry when (*name the apparent cause of the anger*) even though this anger disconnects me from my heart's shen of unconditional love" *(will be on/umb on because client resonates with this anger, which blocks the opening of the heart to love).*

d. **Identify the self-doubt involved**
Ask, "In what way do you doubt yourself, lose your confidence in yourself in relation to (*name person*)?"
*[cr] with "I (*name the self-doubts*), even though my self-doubt disconnects me from my heart's shen of unconditional love" *(will be on/umb on because client resonates with these self-doubts, which block the opening of your heart to love).*

D. Identify the earlier experience of the heart wound
Do {a–f} in sequence.

a. **The experience**
Ask, "What earlier experience do you feel is related to your closing your heart to unconditional love?"
*[cr] with "(*Name the earlier experience in a present-tense statement*) which closes my awareness to unconditional love" *(will be on/umb on because client still resonates with this painful experience that closed awareness of unconditional love).*

b. The negative belief
Ask, "What negative belief about (yourself • men • women • life) did you have concerning love as a result of that experience?"
[cr] (will be on/umb on because client still resonates with believing this thought-belief to be true).

c. The result
Ask, "As a result of (*name the negative belief*) what outcomes do you see in your life?"
[cr] (will be on/umb on because client resonates with this negative result that blocks the opening of the heart to love).

d. Positive belief and result in response to the earlier experience
Write down the belief *{D b}* and result *{D c}* of the earlier experience, but put them in a positive life-affirming statement.
[cr] (will be off/umb off because at the moment client does not resonate with a positive belief and a positive outcome, which open the heart to love).

e. Acceptance of the earlier experience
Understanding acceptance is needed?
Resistance blocks the natural pulsation of your energy, which causes your frequencies to be out of sync or non-coherent. Non-coherence creates pain, difficulties and illness.

The *thoughts* about your earlier experience that you resonate with have become as significant, or perhaps even more significant, than the experience itself.

Negative thoughts continue to create the same pain in the present that you experienced in the past. This makes it impossible for you to let go of the story of that experience, and keeps the possibility for unconditional love a distant dream.

Complete acceptance, free of all resistance, allows your frequencies to return to their natural state of coherence, which opens your heart to limitless possibilities for love in your life.

Write down, "I accept (*name the earlier experience*) free of all resistance and I open my heart so I am receptive to the field of unconditional love." *[cr] (will be off/umb off because client does not resonate with acceptance of the earlier experience, even though non-acceptance closes the heart to unconditional love).*

f. **New memory-thought**
   Ask, "What do you want instead of that memory-frequency that will open your heart to love?" *Explain,* "Everything is in your mind: the earlier experience is over, but you maintain the story of it in your mind, which makes it ever-present, never over. Now, you can create a new frequency and activate a new brain-nerve pathway. So, what do you want instead of that painful memory?"
   [cr] (will be off/umb off because client does not resonate with this new positive memory-thought that opens the heart to love).

E. **Identify the coherent qualities of the Heart Official needed (mcs) {1–21}.**
   [cr] (will be off/umb off because client does not yet resonate with opening his/her awareness to the unconditional love that is the client's true nature).
   1. I stay connected to my heart's love and intuitive knowing and avoid getting angry about anything in this world.
   2. I listen and understand.
   3. (I am a loving presence • I connect with each person I meet in loving friendship).
   4. I have confidence in myself and my inner knowing.
   5. I see (people/*name person*) in a positive light and I use positive words that amplify his/her/their light.
   6. I give whatever love and light I have.
   7. I serve the Divine in all I do.
   8. I share what I have with pleasure.
   9. I remember who I am in my spirit.
   10. I remember who others are in their spirit.
   11. I keep my heart open to love, gratitude and appreciation.

12. I practice the presence of the Divine in all situations.
13. I am protected by unconditional love.
14. (The light of my eyes brings the shen of unconditional love to each person I meet • My heart's shen connects to the heart's shen of (others/ *name person*) and there is nothing but love).
15. I stay connected to the truth of my heart's knowing and live that truth.
16. I allow my life to unfold naturally, doing nothing if necessary.
17. (My heart knows what I need to do and say • I relax into heart silence and allow what is best for me at this time to make itself known).
18. I listen to and act on my conscience.
19. I am fully present in the moment, (listening to my inner truth • connected to my inner light).
20. I focus within.
21. I speak the truth.

F. Identify the action needed for regaining awareness of the creative principle of unconditional love
(**mcs**) {1–10} for the primary one needed at this time.
*[**cr**] (*will be off/umb off*).
1. (I tell the truth • I live the truth).
2. I look into the eyes of (others • *name person*) with unconditional love.
3. I avoid talking negatively about (*name person* • *anyone*).
4. I avoid judging (anyone • *name person*).
5. I listen with understanding.
6. I avoid complaining about anything that happens.
7. I focus on the moment with love and attention.
8. I am a loving presence for (others • *name person*).
9. I remember my heart is the Emperor who brings divine unconditional love and compassion to every relationship.
10. I remember that the heart of (others • *name person involved*) is the Emperor who is filled with divine unconditional love and I see him/her/ them in this light.

G. Identify the smile factor
Read the story of the smiling man *p.14*

Ask, "What does this story mean for you in relation to your heart's intention *{A d}*?" *[**cr**] with "To have (*name {A d}*) I (*name the positive meaning*)" *(will be off/umb off).*

H. Identify the heart action(s) needed in challenging situations and relationships

(**mcs**) {a–f} for the one(s) needed.

a. I consciously relax all tension in (*name the situation*) that creates stress for me.

b. I breathe easily.

c. I create heart connection with (others • *name person involved*) through (my smile • loving touch • kind words • listening with understanding • song • *name something else*).

d. I go into action to support (*name person/others*) handle life positively and with inner strength.

e. I appreciate and accept every circumstances of my life no matter how difficult it is and I move into being of service for (*others/name person*) in whatever way I can.

f. I do my spiritual practice daily, giving it full time with focused, loving attention.

I. The indigenous way of seeing the heart of another: "Kill the enemy"

Ask, "Name all (*name person*)'s good qualities – whatever you like or admire about him/her." *[**cr**] with "I see (*name person*)'s (*name good qualities*). I see his/her spot of light. I see his/her heart. He/She is too good to be my enemy. We are in harmony" *(will be off/umb off).*

J. Identify the Energizing Option needed
Client tones his/her Birth Note to reconnect to the heart

a. **Birth Note toning to reconnect to the heart**
   Explain: Toning notes has a positive impact on the mind and feelings as well as the physical body. Dr. Alfred Tomatis discovered that high-

frequency vocal sounds recharge the brain and toning of notes has been shown to destroy cancer cells and enliven healthy cells.
See ResonanceRepatterning.net e-Store for the chromatic toner

b. **Information needed**
   - Identify the note needed from the Birth Note Chart. Look at the Birth Note Chart and find your four birth notes: the note that corresponds with your birth month, the note that is opposite your birth note (known as the reciprocal) and the two notes on either side of the reciprocal note. If you know how to muscle check, you can (**mcs**) which of these four notes you need to tone. If not, intuitively choose one of these four notes.

   - (**mcs**) for the vowel sound needed (oo • or • ah • eh • ee • or humming). Make the sound nasal.

   - (**mcs**) for the chakra center where you need to feel the sound vibrating: (Base of the Spine • Pelvis • Solar Plexus • Heart • Throat • Brow • Crown) chakra.

   - Identify the color(s) needed for the CYW Lenses. Check if the color(s) relate to any of the birth notes.

c. **How To:**
   - Client puts on CYW Lenses

   - Clients stands and does the chest opening movement: arms extended in front of chest, palms facing. Draw the elbows back and slightly down, in a vigorous movement. Repeat five times.

   - Client sits and with thumbs touches the Heart Meridian acupuncture point, Utmost Source, at the armpit behind the tendon.

   - Client tones or hums his/her birth note (or you may use the tuning fork for the birth note. *See* SPIRAL UP! *for options on how to use the Tuning Forks as an Energizing Option*). (**mcs**) when complete.

- Instead of toning the birth note, RR practitioners may (**mcs**) to use a Tuning Fork for the birth note. Muscle check whether the note of the Tuning Fork needs to be heard (and over which ear), or whether the Tuning Fork needs to be held over a particular Chakra energy center, a vertebra associated with the Chakra center, on an Acupuncture Mu point or other Acupuncture Element point.

d. Resonance Repatterning practitioners will now recheck the *[**cr**] statements and confirm any change in resonance.

BIRTH NOTE CHART

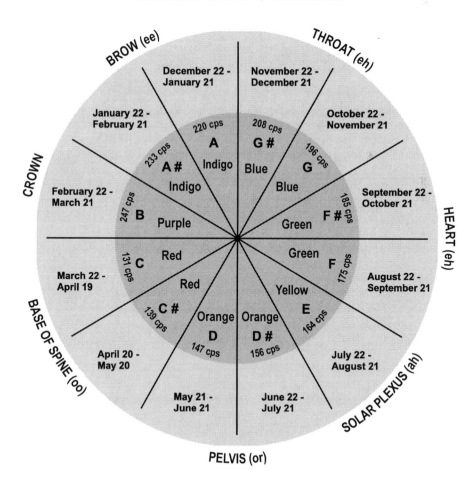

HOW TO USE THE
SEEING THE HEART REPATTERNING
IN YOUR DAILY LIFE
EVEN IF YOU HAVE NOT YET ATTENDED A
RESONANCE REPATTERNING SEMINAR

- Take time to be quiet and alone: relax, breathe and allow yourself to be still physically and to slow down your thoughts as much as your mind allows.

- In stressful situations, remember the old man and the drunkard and the Smiling Man. What can you do to bring love from within yourself in this situation – without words?

- Any time you have a difficult person in your life, check this Repatterning for one or two letters, followed by toning your birth note or doing a SPIRAL UP! Energizing Option, to help you reconnect to your heart and the field of unconditional love. **For instance, just do letter I. and an Energizing Option.**

- You can take a letter that has particular meaning for you, and then do an Energizing Option to change your resonance with the item you have completed.

- Gradually you can do different combinations of the letters in five-ten minute mini-sessions. When you do different combinations like this, your negative resonance for the problem may still show up because you are getting in touch with specific aspects of the overall problem. In relation to those aspects, the resonance with the problem hasn't yet changed. Spiral in gently and be in your process of positive change in a way that is profound, yet easy.

RR SESSIONS: If you would like to receive the complete Repatterning with a professional Resonance Repatterning Practitioner, in person or over the phone, go to ResonanceRepatterning.net > Sessions for RR Institute Practitioners worldwide who have listed themselves on the RRI website.

RR SEMINARS: If you would like to attend Resonance Repatterning seminars in person or online, so you can use RR effectively on yourself and/or others, go to ResonanceRepatterning.net > Seminars for the list of teachers endorsed by the Resonance Repatterning Institute to teach.

2. LISTENING TO THE HEART –
COMMUNICATING FOR CONNECTION

[In the womb – where the ears of the fetus are immersed in liquid – hearing the mother's voice is by bone conduction.]

To hear the mother's voice the baby puts his body against the spinal column, a column of sound. That way he is directly 'plugged in' to the voice. Toward the end of the pregnancy, he puts his head down against the hip bones of the mother, which become his own private auditorium at the bottom of the spine....

This body-to-body connection made by the unborn child in his quest for the mother's voice is his initial attempt to listen. Its significance is tremendous, because it is the first step toward communicating. As the mother's voice comes and goes, the very first desire is born – the desire to hear the voice – and the first gratification [is] the pleasure of receiving it again. Repeated over and over, this desire-pleasure cycle creates a need for communication. Therefore, in the chronology of human needs, the need to reach out and to communicate seems to be the primary one.

Paul Madaule, *When Listening Comes Alive:
A Guide to Effective Learning and Communication*

LISTENING TO HEARTS

A gifted cancer surgeon who was deeply depressed came to Dr. Rachel Remen for counseling. He was disillusioned dealing with the same complaints day after day, seeing the same diseases over and again, and felt cynical – hardly caring any more. He had reached the point where on many days he didn't even want to get out of bed.

Rachel Remen suggested something she had found helpful for people who were going through this kind of dark night: that he review the events of his day and ask himself three questions, and journal his answers. The questions were:

1. What surprised me today?
2. What moved me or touched me today?
3. What inspired me today?

The cancer surgeon laughed, but agreed to try her suggestion – at least, he said, it was cheaper than prozac. In the first few days the results of the questions were non-existent: in response to all three questions his answer was an inevitable 'nothing, nothing, nothing.'

Rachel suggested he start looking at people with new eyes – looking for their stories. Six weeks later the cancer surgeon came in with a little bound book.

Slowly, he said, he had begun to find answers to the three questions – bit by bit seeing a little more deeply, beyond a surprise that a tumor had grown or shrunk, or that a new drug was working. He began to see people "who had found their way through great pain and darkness by following a thread of love … people who had found ways to triumph over pain, suffering and even death."

Gradually, instead of answering the three questions at the end of his day by looking backward, he started to see things as they were happening. This was when he noticed that his attitude had changed and that people were picking up on it. And their attitude toward him was changing too.

He found himself talking to people about more than their cancer. Then he started sharing the strengths he saw in them.

Rachel Remen writes that the first patient he spoke to in this way was a thirty-eight year-old woman with ovarian cancer who had undergone major abdominal surgery, followed by a very debilitating chemotherapy.

In the midst of a routine follow-up visit one morning, he suddenly 'saw' her for the first time – her four-year-old on her lap and her six-year-old leaning against her chair. Both little girls were clean, well fed, happy and obviously well loved.

Aware of the profound suffering caused by her sort of chemotherapy, he was deeply moved by the depth of her commitment to mother her children, and for the first time he connected it to the strength of her will to live.

After they spoke of her symptoms, he commented: "You are such a great mother to your kids. Even after all you have been through, there is something very strong in you. I think that power could maybe heal you some day." She smiled at him, and he realized with a shock that he had never seen her smile before. "Thank you," she told him warmly. "That means a lot to me."

Now he began to ask others, "Where do you find your strength?" and "What sustains you?" For the first time he began to know *people*, not just cancer. And as he changed, his patients did too: people thanked him for their surgery, some gave him gifts.

After a silence, the surgeon brought out a stethoscope engraved with his name that a patient had given him. He was clearly moved by this gift.

Rachel smiled and referring to the stethoscope asked him, "And what do you do with that?" Suddenly he laughed: "I listen to hearts... I listen to hearts."

This is the essence of what communication is all about – an opportunity to listen to the heart of another and share our heart.

If doing the Repatterning, return to {A} p.47

The ideal communication

What we want to experience in every communication, to one extent or another, is mutual pleasure, closeness, acceptance, love and the feeling that we are understood and that we understand, that we 'see' another's essence.

This ideal happens automatically when the pulsing energy frequencies of the heart of both people are in sync, or what is called entrained.

When frequencies are entrained, pulsing in rhythm together like two pendulum clocks swinging in unison, they amplify what is positive. This brings more joy and love to the relationship – whether between two people, intimate partners, a family or any group, and even with someone you say hello to in passing.

Entrainment of frequencies is the key ingredient. The surgeon found a way to entrain with the heart of his patients through his growing interest in them and their strengths. The narrow focus on his patients' disease, which depleted his energy and caused him to distance himself from his patients, stopped him from entraining with their heart and appreciating who they were beyond their illness.

As a result of painful earlier experiences when basic life needs were not met and resolved, we become locked into sympathetic nervous system (SNS) stress reactions. Stress reactions in our relationships and in response to life circumstances creates a loss of balance in our Five Element energies and a disconnect from our heart and the heart of others.

Heart entrainment is missing. Our frequencies are out of sync with others' frequencies. Now there is less energy, less pleasure, less harmony, a feeling of frustration and a sense of disconnection. And when frequencies oppose each other – when they are totally out of sync – there is no positive energy: only anger, quarrels, loss of love and depression.

Fortunately there are practical things we can do to bring our frequencies into sync with others' frequencies – to listen to their heart.

Let's look at ten facets of connection that make listening to the heart possible.

1. **Acknowledging another's presence**

   In Fiji, whenever you pass anyone in the street, even if you pass them again a few minutes later, you always acknowledge this moment of meeting by making eye contact, smiling and saying "Bu-la."

   In India people put the palms of their hands together at their heart or forehead and say "Namaste" – 'I greet the divine within you'. In the West we make eye contact, smile and say "Hello, how are you?"

   These simple words and gestures – eye contact and smiling with pleasure – are the beginning of entraining our frequencies with another's.

   Acknowledgment is about seeing what is good and admirable in each person we meet. This helps bring our frequencies into sync with someone else's frequencies: both energy fields are amplified and we feel good about ourselves and those we meet. As a result, at the end of the day we are still energized and happy.

   If doing the Repatterning, return to {E a} p.54

   If doing the Repatterning, return to {E a} p.54

   ∽

When our frequencies are out of sync, we don't acknowledge another's presence at the moment of meeting. When we don't make eye contact, don't smile and don't greet each other, there is no connection. This is when we feel invisible and alone, because our energy field isn't being amplified.

Sometimes family members come home from work or school and don't take the time to say "bu-la" – to smile, hug, connect. Then husbands and wives, parents and children too, can feel invisible and alone. They feel taken for granted and the relationship suffers – sometimes to the point of separation.

So the first facet in listening to the heart is to acknowledge each meeting, acknowledge another's presence from our heart: I greet the divine within you – eye contact, a smile, a greeting. Or at least silently greet people in our heart if it isn't possible to use words!

2. **Awareness**

As the cancer surgeon became aware, his heart opened. For instance, his awareness of what a good mother his patient was. Our awareness of each other's strengths, positive qualities and the impact these may have on others' lives connects us to the heart of another.

It takes time, observation and practice to become aware of another's strengths. Sharing this awareness of strengths opens the heart. And an open heart leads to yet more awareness and sharing of what we see with empathy, which automatically strengthens and energizes ourself and the other person.

If doing the Repatterning, return to {F a} p.54

〜

3. **Being fully present and questions**

Being fully present is essential if we want to open our heart for authentic connection. If we aren't giving one-pointed attention, genuine listening won't happen. As a consequence, frequency entrainment is canceled out. The heart closes down and may not open so easily the next time you want to connect.

Certain things we do undermine the possibility for a heart connection. For instance, asking a question when our mind is elsewhere, or when we are in a hurry, or when we are multi-tasking, checking emails, texting, answering our iPhone, using our iPad or when we are otherwise distracted. We are not fully focused on listening to the answer to our question. If we are only half-present, entrainment of the heart will not occur.

Some people are willing to share themselves with others if the other person shows an interest by asking questions. Often people enjoy talking about themselves and their life but fail to show a reciprocal interest in others by asking questions that motivate the other person to share their interests and experiences.

Basically, questions are about gathering information. But open questions, which require more than a yes/no answer, tell another person that we want to know more about them, that we are interested in getting to know their strengths, what they have experienced, what helped them through their experiences, what excites them, what dreams and vision they have for their life.

Open questions with deep listening – taking the time to listen with patience and focus – takes a relationship to a deeper level of sharing and an opening of the heart.

If doing the Repatterning, return to {G a} p.55

Questions when frequencies are out of sync

When our frequencies are out of sync with another's frequencies, we are unable to use questions to deepen the relationship. We may find ourselves asking closed questions that only require yes/no answers, but don't lead to any sharing: "Are you feeling good?" Yes/No. "Do you want to eat at this restaurant?" Yes/No. Or the person being questioned may feel they are being grilled or cross-examined.

Married couples who have been together for many years, or colleague relations between a boss and employee, may tend to move into closed yes/no questions that add nothing new to their relationship. It's important for couples, and people in general, to keep practicing open questions so they are always discovering new things about each other.

Discovering new ideas, feelings and responses is what keeps a relationship interesting, growing and alive. Attentive listening to another's responses deepens the relationship.

When our frequencies are out of sync, we may use questions with a hidden (perhaps unconscious) agenda in mind, or even use them as a subtle put-down. When non-innocent questions are asked, we often feel uncomfortable, we may even get reactive or feel confused: what answer are they really wanting from me?

For example, "Did you empty the trash?" may be a question wanting information as a yes/no answer. Or it may have a subtle agenda behind it – a frustration with a partner who said he/she would empty the trash and never does.

It is good to observe how we use questions in our communications. And to observe how comfortable the other person feels.

4. **Similarities and differences**
   Similarities create an instant liking, an attraction, a bond that can lead to friendship and even committed love. When we are similar, we have a natural harmony with another person, we feel aligned. The more alignment, the easier the relationship.

   With our questions we are looking for the similarities that connect us and bring a sense of unity so we feel energized and good about our self and the other person.

   If doing the Repatterning, return to {H a} p.56

   ⌒

A similarity can be quite simple. For instance, if I meet someone who hears my English accent and they say, "Oh, I love England," we have an immediate similarity, a bond and liking. I feel good about myself and the other person, and they feel good about themselves and me! Whereas if I meet someone who says, "I hate England and the English," now we have a difference, a disharmony, a disconnection. We don't feel good about each other, and we'll have to find numerous points of similarity to transcend this one basic difference.

However, some differences can be exciting, in spite of the sense of separation they create. For instance, a husband and wife may have very different interests or points of view that add richness and stimulation to their relationship. They may enjoy different books or movies, even different spiritual paths. As long as they use their differences to create interest and connection rather than disconnection they will maintain and deepen their bond.

5. **Listening with empathy and reflection**
Empathetic listening with reflection involves listening with understanding. When we give our time to this kind of listening with empathy and reflection, we don't need to fix anything, explain anything, interpret anything, give directions or offer advice and solutions. None of these is needed when someone simply wants to talk things out and get some clarity.

Allowing someone in need the freedom to talk without interruption is a great gift. Sometimes the person who is talking may feel guilty because there isn't a reciprocal back-and-forth kind of conversation. Then you need to give reassurance: "It's good for you to talk this out. I'm happy to be here for you as a listening presence."

The result of this kind of communication for connection is that we feel good to have been of service, and the other person feels lighter for having trusted that it is safe to open their heart to share. All of us at one time or another need a listening presence like this.

If doing the Repatterning, return to {I a} p.57

⌀

With empathetic listening we don't do a lot of talking. At a moment of a pause we may offer a short summary of what we are hearing: "You feel scared to tell your boss that you disagree with him." This kind of listening presence gives the other person the space to talk; it helps them get clear on their own thinking and a possible course of action.

This kind of listening, simple as it is, is quite rare. We tend to feel impatient when a friend is going on and on! We often interrupt them or jump in with advice, answers and solutions because we feel the conversation is taking too much time!

If someone needs a listening presence, but we keep offering solutions, they won't hear or follow through on our advice, which makes us feel even more frustrated and impotent. And if they don't feel heard, they generally start repeating themselves, which can make us even more impatient!

When our frequencies are out of sync, we won't be able to listen to people empathetically in their time of need. Instead we multi-task – listen to a friend on the phone while we wash up the dishes, do our emails or make a to do list for the next day. We aren't focused on the person we are listening to. We may be efficient at getting several things done at once, but we have forgotten that focused attention is how we connect to the heart, even when we are talking on the phone. Just because the other person cannot see us doesn't mean we can multi-task and still have a heart connection!

In addition, if we aren't listening empathetically and attentively, we won't be able to reflect back a summary of their thoughts and feelings, and they won't receive the listening that helps them clarify their problem or simply feel heard.

People talk and listen because they want a heart connection. Heart connection is the priority. And when we take the time to listen with empathy and reflection, we are fully available for a connection to take place between two hearts.

6. **Adding meaning**
    Adding meaning happens when we are able to bring a deeper understanding to another person. We see a connection in what they are saying, and at the

right moment we share it – saying, for example, "What I am seeing is that as a child when you came home from boarding school and felt like a stranger, this is quite similar to what's happening now. You travel, and when you come home to your wife and children you feel like a stranger." Adding meaning usually brings an 'aha' moment to the other person: "Wow! I never saw that before!"

We see this kind of connection with the cancer surgeon who added a deeper meaning to his observation that his patient was a great mother. He shared that he felt this strength would help her self-heal. Powerful. And energizing. When we are able to bring a deeper meaning – the 'wow, I never saw that before' – this is often when positive change or self-healing gathers momentum.

If doing the Repatterning, return to {J a} p.58

When our frequencies are in sync within ourselves and with the person we are communicating with, we begin to see meaning more often and become attuned to the right moment for sharing the meaning we perceive. In this way we are able to help the other person see the true answer or insight they are seeking.

Sometimes we may see a deeper meaning, but intuitively stay silent: the time may not be right for sharing our insight, so we contain it.

When our frequencies are out of sync, instead of meaning, we go into diagnosing, analyzing, interpreting and making generalizations, giving solutions, sharing our own experiences, or we may share what we see when the person is not receptive to hearing it – all of which leave us feeling not so good about ourselves or the person we're communicating with.

7. **Advice or feedback**
Advice or feedback is given to encourage another person to modify their behavior and to generate positive change in their thinking or habits. Even if

a suggestion is rejected, it may still lead the other person to move in a new direction, if not now then later. Or the rejected suggestion may take them to a different resolution of their problem.

Giving advice is the mainstay of most relationships because people want advice and most of us love giving it! When a family member takes our advice and adjusts their behavior, it creates similarity, which encourages closeness, reduces conflict and sustains love. Coherent advice that is received and acted on by the other person also supports transformation and growth in the one who hears the advice.

If doing the Repatterning, return to {K a} p.59

⌒

When advice is not received or is outright rejected, we need to be tolerant and take it as an opportunity to rise above our ego self-importance that thinks we have the answer. And perhaps the person needs one of the other facets of connection rather than our focus on #7!

A few ways for giving good advice
When our frequencies are in sync, we give good advice, when asked for and needed. We are able to give advice in different ways according to the situation:

- If unsure, ask, "Would you like to hear what I think might help, or would you like more time to share?"

- We may ask "Why don't you..." questions that gently offer a new possibility.

- We may tell our own story – offering a personal example of what worked for us and therefore might also work for the other person.

- We may offer suggestions: "You could try this..." or "Have you tried...?"

- We may give soft commands – a command with a rationale behind it that affects their behavior: "Go to AA next week and explore how they help with alcohol problems" or "You need to get your act together and start living a moral life."

- Sometimes we may affect another's behavior with a hard command: "Do not cross the road!" to a child, or "Stop labeling me!" to a family member. Hard commands can sound dictatorial because they offer no reason for the command. Just do it! We often use hard commands in conflict situations, which usually escalates the conflict. Better to use them in a life/death situation or when we really need to set a strong boundary.

When our frequencies are out of sync, we offer our advice and solutions when they are not wanted, needed or asked for. Rejection of advice usually happens when we offer advice prematurely before the other person has had a chance to share what is really going on, or before they feel listened to or when we offer advice that doesn't resonate with them. Or perhaps we are giving advice as a substitute for genuine heart connection.

We may also start giving solutions because
- we are not comfortable with being a listening presence for someone

- we may not have the time to listen with focused attention

- we may feel as though quiet listening isn't enough (yin/feminine)

- we may feel that we can only be helpful when we go into action to solve someone's problem (yang/masculine)

Another problem with advice is that it can lead to more conflict and even keep a fight alive: "Why don't you get some help?" might escalate the conflict if the heart connection behind the words is not strong.

For advice to be heard and taken to heart, the person we are advising needs to be receptive to us and asking for advice. They also need to know that we have really listened first, which provides the foundation for knowing or intuiting the kind of advice that might be helpful. Sometimes instead of giving advice it might be more effective to ask a question and simply listen.

8. Reciprocal sharing

When two people share themselves, it leads to closeness and a deepening bond. And deep bonds of closeness always involve two people reciprocally sharing themselves – either one after the other or one person at one time and the other person at another time.

When there is trust and commitment in a relationship, we share our personal life experiences, our pain, our joys, our moments of magic. And when we have established a bond of trust, then there may be reciprocal sharing of mistakes made and regrets and talking about the most meaningful experiences of our life.

Reciprocal sharing needs to be matched. If one person is sharing their response to a political rally, for example, it is probably not the time to reveal a dark secret from our past! Unmatched sharing doesn't lead to closeness. When sharing is matched, it leads to trust and a gradually deepening bond.

In every relationship there is an appropriate time to reveal ourselves, based on the level of trust established over time with the other person. Step by step we reveal ourselves and share our secrets.

Risky disclosures need to be preceded by many safer disclosures. As less risky disclosures lead to more intimacy, we trust that we are safe to be vulnerable and reveal more of our inner life – at each stage checking that we are still accepted and loved.

Without sharing, or disclosures, there is no intimacy. This is why we take the risk to be honest with each other and to reveal ourselves.

If doing the Repatterning, return to {L a} p.61

∽

If only one person shares on a consistent basis, this one-sided sharing does not lead to mutual closeness. The relationship then becomes at best a therapeutic one. One-sided sharing that continues over days, weeks and months may lead to frustration, withdrawal and a sense that mutual caring and friendship is lacking.

But sometimes a friend is in trouble and they simply don't have the focus or energy to listen reciprocally to what is going on with us. As long as we understand and accept this situation, we will be able to maintain the connection in spite of the lack of mutual sharing.

Reciprocal sharing may begin with talking about the weather – an initial entrainment of frequencies. This may lead to sharing something about our day. Then we share ideas or feelings or something we are excited about.

When a partner or friend responds with focused attention, love, understanding and acceptance, it opens the way for yet more sharing on both sides.

When frequencies are out of sync, we may not resonate with revealing ourselves at all. Total withholds put a ceiling on closeness and obstruct the growth of a deepening intimacy.

Out-of-sync frequencies can also lead us to reveal our pains and mistakes prematurely, before trust and safety have been established in the relationship. This can lead to rejection, even to the break-up of a relationship – temporary or permanent – and betrayal too, if the information is misused or a confidence is not honored.

Relationship is about sharing our wonderful moments that are deeply meaningful, as well feeling free to share our unvarnished truths – our embarrassing moments, hilarious experiences, private thoughts, romantic feelings, and mistakes too – trusting that our sharing will be honored and we are still loved.

Our fear that we won't be loved and accepted if someone knows our soft spots has to be faced. When we unveil our inner life with those we trust, and they receive what we share with love, understanding or appropriate humor, it opens our heart so more love flows and the intimacy deepens.

9. Silence

Silence regulates the rhythm of listening and talking.

Silence allows a person to go deeper into their feelings, thoughts and sharing.

Fast-paced talk survives on little or no silence between one person talking and the next. The lack of silence often stops a deeper sharing in its tracks.

Being comfortable with silence is essential for the expression of deeper emotions, creative ideas and personal disclosures.

Longer wait times between taking turns, without rushing our response, without interrupting or talking over someone, makes people feel listened to. It creates trust and helps another person share more deeply what is on their mind or hidden in their heart.

Becoming comfortable with silence takes practice: breathing slowly through the nose, relaxing deeply, staying present and attentive to the other person and slowing down the speed at which we talk. Relaxed and understanding eye contact helps in this learning process.

If doing the Repatterning, return to {M a} p.64

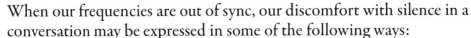

When our frequencies are out of sync, our discomfort with silence in a conversation may be expressed in some of the following ways:

- We feel tense and stop breathing.

- We talk too quickly.

- We break eye contact and disconnect.

- We may only be focused on talking, showing no interest in asking questions that get the other person sharing and talking.

- We fill in every pause with chatter of any kind or quality.

- We cut off another person's sharing prematurely by responding with our own thoughts or experiences.

- We interrupt and may even talk over the other person.

- We seem interested in another person's sharing, but then become easily distracted, which puts a stop to the sharing or a deepening connection.

- We start playing with our iPhone, iPad or computer.

- We jump in with our own experience or idea that the other person's sharing triggers in us – and the person lapses into silence at this take-over, feeling we are not really interested in hearing what they have to say.

- We may end the conversation prematurely and move on to talk to someone else before the conversation has time to go deeper or before it is complete. When we leave conversations too early, we feel uncomfortable: we know the connection didn't happen. It's as though a firework was lit and then fizzled out. And we try to avoid thinking about the part we played in the fizzle.

The natural back-and-forth of conversation doesn't happen without pauses for silence. The closer we become with another, the more comfortable we are with silence. We know the time to speak and the time to simply be there with each other.

10. Make amends for mistakes

Atonement means 'at one' and also means to make amends. When our frequencies are in sync, we recognize when we have made a mistake and we want to apologize or ask for forgiveness so once more we can feel 'at one.'

None of us is perfect, and when we are genuinely sorry for what we have said and done, or not said and done, the other person is usually quick to forgive. Separation, disunity and a lack of forgiveness fill us with regret, and if not rectified can make us ill and create great unhappiness in our relationships.

If doing the Repatterning, return to {N a} p.65

⌒

When our frequencies are out of sync:
- we refuse to recognize that we have made a mistake

- we blame others for our upsets and even for our own mistakes

- we justify our actions so as to prove in our own eyes that we are right and the other person is wrong

- we don't say sorry

- if we do say sorry, it gets turned around into indirect statements like "I'm sorry you feel hurt," instead of the more direct and genuine "I'm sorry I hurt you with my criticism"

- we close the lines of communication – we cut off the communication, rather than share feelings and needs

Summary of the ten facets for communicating for connection
1. Acknowledging someone's presence.
2. Noticing what is good or a strength in another
3. Open questions
4. Similarities and differences
5. Listening with empathy and reflection
6. Adding meaning
7. Giving advice
8. Reciprocal sharing
9. Silence
10. Making amends

These ten facets are the foundation for listening to the heart that supports continued love and respect in every good relationship. The Repatterning helps us resonate with the qualities of listening to the heart by using these ten facets. We'll also change our resonance with out-of-sync frequencies that reinforce disconnection from our own heart and the heart of another.

FURTHER READING

Gerald Goodman, PhD and Glenn Esterly. *The Talk Book: The Intimate Science of Communicating in Close Relationships.*

Michael Kahn, PhD. *The Tao of Conversation: How to Talk about Things that Really Matter, in Ways that Encourage New Ideas, Deepen Intimacy, and Build Effective and Creative Working Relationships.*

Paul Madaule. *When Listening Comes Alive: A Guide to Effective Learning and Communication.*

Rachel Naomi Remen, MD. *My Grandfather's Blessings: Stories of Strength, Refuge, and Belonging.*

2. LISTENING TO THE HEART REPATTERNING

A. Read or tell the story of the cancer surgeon *p.27*
Ask, "What does this story mean for you?" *[cr] with "I (*name the positive meaning*)" (*will be off/umb off*).

B. Name the problem with communicating and connection
Do (a–d) in sequence.
a. *Ask,* "Who do you have a problem communicating with or feeling connected to? What's the problem with your communication with (*name the person*)?"
*[cr] (*will be on/umb on because client resonates with having a problem communicating with the person and feeling a sense of connection with his/her heart*).

b. (**mcs**) We need to identify if your (partner • mother • father • family member • friend • colleague • people in general • someone else) are also involved with this communication and connection problem?" *Ask,* "What is the problem with your communication with (*name the person/people*)?" *[cr] (*will be on/umb on*).

c. *Ask,* "How do you feel in response to this difficulty in communicating and connecting with (*name the person(s) in {a–b}*)?" *[cr] (*will be on/umb on*).

d. *Ask,* "How would you like your communication to be?" *[cr] with "I (*name the new way of communicating wanted*)" (*will be off/umb off*).

C. Identify the past unmet need that underlies the connection problem
(**mcs**) (1–5) for the need category
1. **The need for security and survival**
   (**mcs**) {1–9}. *[cr] (*will be off/umb off*).
   1. (I am cared for • I am looked after • My Life Needs are met).

2. I feel secure.
3. Everything is provided for.
4. (I survive • I am successful).
5. I am protected.
6. I have a home. I am clothed, fed and kept warm.
7. (I am welcomed • I belong).
8. Other: *Ask,* "What do you need in order to feel secure about your survival?"

2. **Physical needs for health and energy**
   (**mcs**) {1–10}. *[cr] *(will be off/umb off)*.
   1. I take in and appreciate living food (mother's milk • fresh homegrown fruits and vegetables • pure water).
   2. I breathe pure air.
   3. (I am warm • I receive the warmth of the sun).
   4. (I move for life • I am energized by movement).
   5. I sleep well and wake up refreshed.
   6. I receive all the (sunlight • full-spectrum light) I need.
   7. I do those actions that lead to health and energy.
   8. I think positive thoughts and feel good about myself and others.
   9. I relax and rejuvenate myself.
   10. Other: *Ask,* "What do you need for your health and energy?"

3. **The need to achieve your best, go beyond your limits and manifest your potential**
   (**mcs**) {1–12}. *[cr] *(will be off/umb off)*.
   1. (I achieve my best • I value those who help me achieve my best).
   2. (I manifest my potential • I am successful • I enjoy going beyond the limits of what I thought was possible).
   3. I have the strength and faith to persevere through obstacles and apparent failures.
   4. I serve (others • humanity).
   5. I play (joyfully • spontaneously).
   6. I am curious.

7. (I create beauty • I am creative in everything I do).
8. I am confident.
9. I am courageous.
10. I maintain an optimistic attitude no matter what difficulties I'm facing.
11. I put my concern for human well-being and right action before my need for (material success • the achievement of my ambitions).
12. Other: *Ask,* "What do you need that would allow you to manifest your potential, go beyond the limits of what you think is possible and achieve your best?"

4. **The need for love and respect in relationship**
   (**mcs**) {1–19}. *[**cr**] *(will be off/umb off).*
   1. I (receive love • give love • feel worthy of being loved) in my relationship with (*name person*).
   2. I have (close • affectionate • caring) relationships.
   3. I belong and feel (welcomed • included • wanted).
   4. I am enough.
   5. I make loving connections through warm and relaxed eye contact.
   6. I give and receive loving touch.
   7. I am protected from harm.
   8. I have clear safe boundaries • I feel safe.
   9. I am (appreciated • acknowledged • valued • respected • accepted).
   10. I enjoy harmonious relationships.
   11. (I have positive communication in my relationship(s) • I am heard • I hear).
   12. (I am seen • I see).
   13. I freely express my (truth • feelings • thoughts • ideas • humor).
   14. I (relax and laugh • enjoy humor).
   15. I am free to explore and return for loving touch and bonding whenever I need to.
   16. My heart is open to (compassion • understanding • love).
   17. (I forgive • I am forgiven • I resolve problems and grow in my capacity to love).

18. I let go of (reactiveness • blame • complaints • feeling a victim • gossip).
19. Other: *Ask,* "What do you need that would bring you love and respect in your relationship(s)?"

5. **The need for meaning, purpose, love, and happiness from within (mcs) {1–20}.** *[cr] *(will be off/umb off).*
    1. (I feel joyful • I let go of all negative thoughts and tune in to love).
    2. I am filled with gratitude every day.
    3. (I see beauty • I see the Divine) in every aspect of the creation.
    4. I am content.
    5. (I have faith • I trust that every experience is for my highest good).
    6. I am (focused • disciplined).
    7. (I pay attention to my thoughts and the stillness of my mind • I am still).
    8. I accept the divine will, free of resistance and fear.
    9. I live my (truth • values) in action.
    10. I love unconditionally.
    11. (I stand for what is right • I live with integrity).
    12. (I practice the presence of God • I feel spiritually connected at all times to the Divine within).
    13. I let go of (self-importance • negative thoughts and feelings).
    14. (I am at peace • My mind is peaceful).
    15. (I am receptive to divine grace).
    16. (I serve selflessly • I give generously • I find every opportunity to help others).
    17. I stay conscious of the light within and the light within each person I meet.
    18. I am receptive to the higher purpose and meaning of every circumstance life brings.
    19. I let go of my need to get (upset • angry) about anything in this world.
    20. Other: *Ask,* "What do you need for your spiritual well-being?"

D. **(mcs)** We need to identify the chronic SNS (sympathetic nervous system) stress response being activated and causing the inability to communicate for connection in the relationship?
(**mcs**) {1–3} for the one involved.
1. **The alert response**
    a. **(mcs)** We need to identify the past **non-coherent** alert neural pathway being reactivated in the present situation that client still resonates with?
        (**mcs**) {1–7}. *[**cr**] *(will be on/umb on)*.
        1. I (freeze • am incapable of action • am paralyzed).
        2. I am inappropriately triggered into a hyper-aroused state.
        3. I (hide • isolate myself) because life is so dangerous.
        4. I am startled by (small things • anything).
        5. I can't relax because I can't (see who or what is dangerous • locate the source of a danger).
        6. I am on the alert for danger all the time.
        7. I am tense all the time.

    b. **(mcs)** We need to identify the **coherent** alert response (*Client*) needs to resonate with in order to create a new neural pathway that supports connection in the present relationship?
        (**mcs**) {1–12}. *[**cr**] *(will be off/umb off)*.
        1. I am alert and ready for action.
        2. I am alert yet relaxed.
        3. I orient myself away from danger.
        4. I orient myself toward what is nourishing, bonding and supports my survival.
        5. I am curious.
        6. If no threat is present, I immediately relax.
        7. I quickly locate where there is danger and who is involved.
        8. I am confident.
        9. I am able to identify and meet any challenge.
        10. I access a wide range of options and reactions.

11. If there is no threat, I release residual activated energy by moving, trembling or shaking out.
12. I easily move through states of tense hyper-vigilance and relaxed alertness.

2. **The fight response**
   a. (**mcs**) We need to identify the past **non-coherent** fight neural pathway client still resonates with? (**mcs**) {1–12}.
      *[**cr**] *(will be on/umb on)*.
      1. (I am defensive • I overreact).
      2. I am overly assertive.
      3. (I am quarrelsome • I pick quarrels).
      4. I am (impatient • angry • frustrated • enraged).
      5. I easily become violent.
      6. I am hyper-nervous.
      7. I am a caretaker for everyone.
      8. I am (over-controlling • dominating).
      9. (I am excessively talkative • I interrupt (*name person*) before he/she has finished talking).
      10. (I make others wrong • I tell (*name person*) that he/she is wrong).
      11. I use sex to discharge my anger.
      12. I can't keep still.

   b. (**mcs**) We need to identify the **coherent** fight response client needs to resonate with in order to create a new neural pathway that supports connection in the present relationship?
      (**mcs**) {1–5}. *[**cr**] *(will be off/umb off)*.
      1. I (defend myself appropriately • set clear boundaries with (clarity • strength • confidence • love).
      2. I stand on my own two feet.
      3. I am ready to face any challenge with (clarity • focused attention • appropriate decision-making • excitement • the ability to see all sides of the situation).
      4. After meeting a challenge I dissipate any residual, mobilized energy by (shaking • trembling • moving • walking • dancing).

5. I share my success in handling a challenge with (*name person*), and I relax into love-bonding once more.

3. **The flight response**
   a. (**mcs**) We need to identify the past **non-coherent** flight neural pathway (*Client*) still resonates with? (**mcs**) {1–10}. *[**cr**] *(will be on/ umb on)*.
      1. (I am unable to avoid dangerous situations • I habitually put myself in dangerous situations).
      2. I run away from situations in a panic, unable to think clearly.
      3. (I get in a panic • I am chronically anxious).
      4. I turn to (food • alcohol • drugs • cigarettes • sex • sleep • day-dreaming • gambling • other) as a way to escape.
      5. (I become ill as a way to avoid a threatening situation • I run away from life).
      6. I stop (hearing • seeing • tasting • smelling • feeling).
      7. I escape by being depressed.
      8. (I can't get going • I can't move into action • I can't (run away • avoid danger).
      9. I cry as a way of handling any emotionally-charged situation I can't cope with.
      10. (I feel threatened • I feel I am in danger • I am hypervigilant • I feel unsafe).

   b. (**mcs**) We need to identify the **coherent** flight response client needs to resonate with in order to create a new neural pathway for connection in the present relationship? (**mcs**) {1–4}. *[**cr**] *(will be off/umb off)*.
      1. I move away from dangerous situations.
      2. I am clear and oriented when facing a danger so I know the best way to handle the difficulty.
      3. After successfully avoiding a threat, I (shake • tremble • move) in order to dissipate any residual mobilized energy.
      4. After successfully avoiding a threat, I discharge excess mobilized energy by playing out different ways of successfully avoiding a challenging situation and I share my success with others.

E. Heart Connection #1: (mcs) Acknowledging another's presence is needed?

    a. **Read the indented paragraphs** #1 *p.31*
       Ask, "What does this mean in relation to your communication issue?"
       *[**cr**] in a positive statement *(will be off/umb off)*.

    b. **(mcs) Coherent acknowledging is needed?**
       (**mcs**) {1–4}. *[**cr**] *(will be off/umb off)*.
       1. I make loving eye contact with (*name person*/those I meet), I smile and I greet him/her/them.
       2. When I pass strangers I feel the equivalent of, 'I greet the Divine within you.'
       3. I see what is good and admirable in each person I meet.
       4. My energy and the energy of any person I acknowledge are amplified with good feelings.

    c. **(mcs) A lack of acknowledging another's presence is involved?**
       (**mcs**) {1–5}. *[**cr**] *(will be on/umb on)*.
       1. I don't make eye contact with those I meet and I don't greet them.
       2. I say 'How are you' by rote, without any heart connection.
       3. (*Name person*) feels invisible to me and I do nothing to acknowledge him/her from my heart.
       4. I feel invisible and alone because (*name person*) doesn't acknowledge me and I feel like I don't exist for him/her.
       5. In my family group we fail to give and receive acknowledgment when we first see each other.

F. Heart Connection #2: (mcs) Awareness of a person's strengths and what is good about them is needed?

    a. **Read the indented paragraphs** #2 *p.32*
       Ask, "What does this mean in relation to your communication issue?"
       *[**cr**] in a positive statement *(will be off/umb off)*.

b. **(mcs) Coherent awareness of another's strengths is needed?**
(**mcs**) {1–3}. *[**cr**] *(will be off/umb off)*.
   1. I notice (*name person*)'s good qualities and strengths.
   2. I share (*name person*)'s good qualities and strengths with him/her.
   3. I share what I appreciate about (*name person*).

c. **(mcs) A lack of awareness of another's strengths is involved?**
(**mcs**) {1–2}. *[**cr**] *(will be off/umb off)*.
   1. I don't notice (*name person*)'s good qualities and strengths.
   2. I notice (*name person*)'s good qualities, but I don't share them with him/her.

G. Heart Connection #3: (mcs) Open questions is needed?

a. **Read the indented paragraphs** #3 *p.32*
Ask, "What does this mean in relation to your communication issue?"
*[**cr**] in a positive statement *(will be off/umb off)*.

b. **(mcs) Appropriate open questions are needed?**
(**mcs**) {1–7}. *[**cr**] *(will be off/umb off)*.
   1. I ask open-ended questions that give (*name person*) a chance to share more and for me to learn more.
   2. My questions stimulate an interesting communication.
   3. My questions let (*name person*/others) know that I am interested in getting to know them.
   4. My questions take our relationship to a deeper level so we feel closer.
   5. Through my questions we discover what we have in common and our similarities create a bond between us.
   6. The similarities we discover as a result of our reciprocal questions and sharing are energizing and pleasurable.
   7. When my questions uncover differences, I stay open and non-judgmental and trust that we can explore our differences for a deeper understanding and harmony.

c. **(mcs) A lack of questions is involved?**
   (**mcs**) {1–5}. *[**cr**] *(will be on/umb on).*
   1. (I ask closed questions that only need yes/no answers • My closed questions fail to open up the communications in an interesting way).
   2. I don't discover anything new about the people I meet/I am with because I am not curious and creative in my questions.
   3. I use questions to disguise subtle criticisms, put-downs or for my own agenda.
   4. I ask interesting questions, but (I am not fully present for listening to the response • I multi-task while listening • I am distracted by my iPhone/iPad/computer/other people • I am not comfortable with silence • I interrupt • I immediately start sharing my own experiences).
   5. I ask factual questions, which fail to stimulate the sharing of ideas or to deepen the bond of closeness.

H. Heart Connection #4: (mcs) Similarities and differences is needed?

a. **Read the indented paragraphs #4** *p.34*
   Ask, "What does this mean in relation to your communication issue?"
   *[**cr**] in a positive statement *(will be off/umb off).*

b. **(mcs) Finding similarities and dealing appropriately with differences is needed?**
   (**mcs**) {1–7}. *[**cr**] *(will be off/umb off).*
   1. I enjoy discovering points of interest and similarities with *(name person/*people).
   2. I feel a natural bond and harmony when I discover similarities in common with *(name person/*people)
   3. I remain interested in *(name person/*people) and non-judgmental when we have different (points of view • interests • religious ideas • political ideas).
   4. Different interests and ways of seeing things add richness to my relationship with *(name person/*people).
   5. Different interests add stimulation and excitement to my relationship with *(name person/*people).

6. I use different ideas and interests to create connection with (*name person*/people).
7. I enjoy exploring our differences together.

c. **(mcs) Non-coherence with finding similarities and dealing appropriately with differences is involved?**
   (**mcs**) {1–5}. *[**cr**] (*will be on/umb on*).
   1. I don't find any points of interest with (*name person*/people).
   2. I cut off from (*name person*/people) because of our differences.
   3. In spite of the similarities with (*name person*/people) our relationship (doesn't feel aligned • doesn't lead to a closer bond).
   4. I don't take the time or give the energy to discover points of interest and similarities with (*name person*/people) and the bond doesn't (happen • deepen).
   5. I feel de-energized by the differences with (*name person*/people) rather than (have a sense of humor about our differences • feel stimulated by our differences • overlook our differences • be patient/tolerant in relation to our differences).

I. **Heart Connection #5: (mcs) listening with empathy and reflection is needed?**

a. **Read the indented paragraphs #5** *p.35*
   Ask, "What does this mean in relation to your communication issue?"
   *[**cr**] in a positive statement (*will be off/umb off*).

b. **(mcs) Listening with empathy and reflection is needed?**
   (**mcs**) {1–8}. *[**cr**] (*will be off/umb off*).
   1. I am patient when (*name person*) needs to talk his/her mind and heart out.
   2. I understand that (*name person*) needs to talk out what is on their mind until they get a sense of clarity.
   3. I am happy to listen with empathy and attention and summarize major thoughts or feelings now and then.

4. I am mostly silent, but when needed I easily reflect back major thoughts and feelings to encourage (*name person*) to share and get clear about what is on their mind and heart.
5. I respond appropriately by recognizing the difference between someone needing an empathetic ear, and someone who is interested in a reciprocal sharing with me.
6. I maintain a balance between listening and sharing with (*name person*/people).
7. If (*name person*/people) is troubled and needs a listening ear, I am happy to offer this and let go of my need for reciprocal sharing.
8. I listen with empathy and awareness of my feelings.

c. **(mcs) A lack of listening with empathy is involved?**
   (mcs) {1–8}. *[cr] *(will be on/umb on).*
   1. I judge (*name person*) when he/she goes into long-drawn-out talking.
   2. I get impatient when (*name person*) is talking about something on their mind, and appears to want nothing from me.
   3. I criticize (*name person*) in my mind as I listen to him/her.
   4. I interrupt (*name person*)'s train of thought.
   5. I interrupt (*name person*)'s communication by offering advice and solutions he/she hasn't asked for and is not interested in hearing at this time.
   6. I feel resentful that (*name person*) is only interested in talking and has no interest in what I would like to share.
   7. I feel like I am stuck in a therapeutic relationship with (*name person*/people), with me listening and him/her/them not interested in listening to what I would like to share.
   8. I (diagnose • analyze • interpret • share my own experiences • give solutions) instead of listening first and discovering what the person is receptive to hearing from me.

J. Heart Connection #6: (mcs) adding meaning is needed?
   a. **Read the indented paragraphs** #6 *p.36*
      Ask, "What does this mean in relation to your communication issue?"
      *[cr]** in a positive statement *(will be off/umb off).*

b. **(mcs) Adding coherent meaning is needed?**
(**mcs**) {1–4}. *[**cr**] *(will be off/umb off).*
1. I bring a deeper understanding to *(name person)* through our communication.
2. I see the connection between one thing and another and share it with *(name person)* at the right moment so he/she sees their experience in a new light.
3. I see *(name person)*'s strengths, share what I see and the deeper meaning their strength could have for them.
4. I listen with attention and understanding and share my perceptions for the benefit of *(name person)* and our mutual learning and appreciation.

c. **(mcs) Adding non-coherent meaning is involved?**
(**mcs**) {1–4}. *[**cr**] *(will be on/umb on).*
1. I diagnose *(name person)* and his/her problem.
2. I analyze *(name person)* and feel superior in my knowledge.
3. I interpret what *(name person)* shares with me instead of letting him/her come to their own understanding.
4. I make generalizations that leave me and *(name person)* feeling empty.

K. Heart Connection #7: (mcs) advice and feedback is needed?

a. **Read the indented paragraphs** #7 *p.37*
Ask, "What does this mean in relation to your communication issue?"
*[**cr**] in a positive statement *(will be off/umb off).*

b. **(mcs) Coherent advice or feedback is needed?**
(**mcs**) {1–9}. *[**cr**] *(will be off/umb off).*
1. I give advice that helps *(name person)* generate positive change he/she needs, wants and is ready for.
2. I receive advice and make adjustments in my habits and behaviors that are good for me and my relationship.
3. I receive and act on the advice that I find helpful.
4. I give advice in a way that it can be heard by *(name person)* and opens new possibilities for him/her.

5. Even if my suggestions are rejected, I trust they may stimulate thinking in a new and helpful direction.
6. I give advice when (*name person*) is receptive to me and my wisdom.
7. I avoid giving advice if (there is no heart connection • I haven't first listened deeply to (*name person*) • (*Name person*) simply needs to talk things out • I don't ask (*name person*) if my suggestion interests them).
8. I listen, provide helpful information and raise questions that clarify the pros and cons of the options, and help (*name person*) arrive at an answer he/she wants to live with.
9. I empower people to make their own decisions by giving helpful feedback.

c. (**mcs**) **Non-coherent advice or feedback is involved?**
(**mcs**) {1–10}. *[**cr**] (*will be on/umb on*).

1. I give advice that is not helpful.
2. I give advice unasked, when it is not wanted or even needed.
3. I give advice when (*name person*) is not receptive to me and my wisdom.
4. Instead of being a peaceful listening presence, I prematurely jump into giving solutions.
5. Instead of asking questions and getting more information about what the person really needs, I jump into giving advice.
6. I use advice inappropriately during a conflict and it creates even more disharmony.
7. Instead of listening, I cut to the chase and tell (*name person*) what I think he/she should do.
8. I give advice based on my own agenda of (worry • fear • upset • other).
9. (I make (*name person*)'s decision for him/her • I interfere in (*name person*)'s destiny/own development/decision-making process) by telling him/her what to do).
10. I give advice instead of simply being in relationship with (*name person/others*).

L. Heart Connection #8: (mcs) reciprocal sharing is needed?

a. Read the indented paragraphs #8 *p.40*
Ask, "What does this mean in relation to your communication issue?"
*[cr] in a positive statement *(will be off/umb off).*

b. (mcs) Reciprocal sharing is needed?
(**mcs**) {1–25}. *[**cr**] *(will be off/umb off).*

1. I honestly share what I feel and need and what is important to me.
2. I listen when (*name person*) shares what he/she feels and needs and what is important to him/her.
3. I think clearly and share my thoughts that lead to new and creative possibilities.
4. I avoid arguments by giving (*name person*) the right to his/her own opinion and perceptions, while respecting my own opinion and perceptions.
5. When I feel demeaned, I am free of reactiveness. I simply share how I feel.
6. When I am disrespected, I ask for information on what I have done that warrants their reaction to me.
7. I do not allow myself to be abused. If necessary I remove myself from the abusive situation.
8. I enjoy discussing different points of view with the understanding that no decision needs to be made and no one is either right or wrong.
9. I avoid arguments because (I accept that we have our own perceptions that are right for us • I am free of a win/lose right/wrong attitude).
10. (I listen and acknowledge (*name person*)'s point of view • I am heard and my point of view is acknowledged).
11. As trust is established (I share my feelings, needs, interests and what I am excited about with (*name person*) • (*Name person*) shares his/her feelings, needs, interests and what he/she is excited about with me).
12. I share my truth at the appropriate time and in a way that (*name person*) receives and values.
13. (I acknowledge and understand (*name person*)'s pain and hurt • (*Name person*) acknowledges and understands my pain and hurt).

14. I avoid all judgments and labeling.
15. I help (*name person*) to clarify his/her ideas and I support new learning and creative options.
16. (*Name person involved*) helps me clarify my ideas and supports new learning and creative options.
17. I share my honest feelings, needs and responses, and I also see and validate (*name person*)'s point of view.
18. I am honest about my needs while reassuring (*name person*) that I also hear his/her needs.
19. I enjoy the back and forth of sharing and listening.
20. When we have a difference of opinion over a decision, we get clear on the issue, then focus on each other's different needs and interests, and discover the best option that respects both of our needs.
21. Through mutual sharing with love and understanding, the bond of love with (*name person*) deepens.
22. I share my (pains • joys • life experiences • mistakes • regrets • moments of magic) with (n*ame person*), appropriate to the trust we have established through our mutual sharing over time.
23. (*Name person*) shares his/her (pains • joys • life experiences • mistakes • regrets • moments of magic) with me, appropriate to the trust we have established through our mutual sharing over time.
24. I respond with (focused attention • love • understanding • acceptance) when (*name person*) (reveals him/herself • shares a risky disclosure • tells the truth about him/herself).
25. (*Name person*) responds with (focused attention • love • understanding • acceptance) when (I reveal myself • I share a risky disclosure • I tell the truth about myself).

c. **(mcs) Lack of reciprocal sharing is involved?**
   (mcs) (1–21). *[**cr**] *(will be on/umb on)*.
   1. I don't share my feelings, needs, opinions and what's important to me.
   2. I don't listen when (*name person*) shares his/her feelings, needs, opinions and what's important to him/her.
   3. I don't have a reciprocal give-and-take in sharing myself and in (*name person*) sharing him/herself.

4. I disclose my mistakes and regrets prematurely, before love and trust have been established and (I get hurt • I feel rejected • the relationship goes off track).

5. My relationship with (*name person*) is out of balance because I share big disclosures before (trust has been established • sharing smaller disclosures that establish a bond of trust • (*Name person*) has shared matching disclosures and built a bond of trust with me).

6. I share my problems and complaints, but don't share my joys, humor, success and magical life-moments.

7. I stop deeper sharing by interrupting or speaking over (*name person*).

8. I am stuck in needing to win and to be right, which blocks deeper sharing with (*name person*).

9. I am stuck in arguments, conflicts and fighting, which blocks deeper sharing.

10. I am reactive in my anger and fear, which obstructs clear thinking and communication with (*name person*).

11. I argue, project, label and get defensive and the bond of love fails to grow.

12. I don't validate (*name person*)'s feelings and good ideas, which stops continued sharing on his/her part.

13. Trust and mutual sharing are destroyed because I go into counter-blame and criticism and justify my actions when I feel criticized.

14. I feel lonely and isolated.

15. I tell (*name person*) how he/she is feeling rather than listen to how he/she is feeling.

16. I am stuck in my position that I am right and (*name person*) is wrong), and we lose our friendship and genuine closeness.

17. When we have a difference of opinion over a decision, I am stuck in my position of what I think is right and we begin to separate from each other.

18. I don't trust that (*name person*/other) is really interested in me, so I don't open up and share myself.

19. I am afraid that if I reveal (myself • my pain • my mistakes • my romantic feelings) (*name person*) will (reject me • no longer love and respect me • withdraw).

20. I don't reveal my (mistakes • regrets • meaningful life experiences • hilarious/embarrassing experiences • needs • what excites me • romantic feelings • moments of magic) with (*name person*) and our bond doesn't deepen.

21. (*Name person*) doesn't reveal his/her (mistakes • regrets • meaningful life experiences • hilarious/embarrassing experiences • needs • what excites him/her • romantic feelings • moments of magic) with me and our bond doesn't deepen.

M. Heart Connection #9: (mcs) relaxed silence in conversation is needed?

a. **Read the indented paragraphs** #9 *p.42*
Ask, "What does this mean in relation to your communication issue?"
*[**cr**] in a positive statement *(will be off/umb off)*.

b. **(mcs) Coherent silence in conversation is needed?**
(**mcs**) {1–8}. *[**cr**] *(will be off/umb off)*.
   1. I am relaxed taking silent pauses mid-sentence or between taking turns in talking and listening, or or when I need to think or (*name person/other*) needs to think.
   2. I am totally at ease with silence in communications as it supports the rhythm of listening and talking.
   3. I am relaxed and at ease with long silences when (*name person*) (is sharing deeper emotional issues • needs to reflect more deeply • needs quietness and to be internal).
   4. I am free of the need to rush my responses or rush (others'/*name person*)'s responses.
   5. I listen to the inner rhythm and pacing of talking and being silent.
   6. I avoid interrupting as a way to avoid silence.
   7. I breathe slowly, relax deeply and stay present with understanding eye contact during a silence in my communication with (*name person/others*).

8. I breathe and allow for silence as a way for (*name person*/other) to get in touch with and express (deeper emotions • creative ideas • a personal disclosure • a deeper sharing of what is on his/her mind and heart).

c. **(mcs) Non-coherent silence is involved?**
(**mcs**) {1–7}. *[**cr**] *(will be on/umb on).*
1. I am not at ease with silence when I communicate with (*name person*/other*).*
2. When there is a silence (I tense up • I feel embarrassed • I can't keep eye contact) and the conversation fizzles.
3. I disconnect or walk away when there is a silence.
4. I avoid silence and keep the conversation going by interrupting or talking over (*name person*/other).
5. I fill in a silence with (meaningless chatter • unnecessary talking).
6. The natural back-and-forth of communication doesn't happen because I don't allow for the natural silence that allows for a deeper sharing.
7. Because of my fear of silence in communication, I lose my confidence when I am with others.

N. **Heart Connection #10: (mcs) Atonement / amends is needed?**
a. **Read the indented paragraphs** #10 *p.43*
Ask, "What does this mean in relation to your communication issue?"
*[**cr**] in a positive statement *(will be off/umb off).*

b. **(mcs) Coherent amends is needed?**
(**mcs**) {1–2}. *[**cr**] *(will be off/umb off).*
1. I recognize when I have made a mistake and I rectify it by communicating what I did and apologizing.
2. When I have done something that creates separation and disunity, (I keep the lines of communication open with (*name person*/other) and create possibilities for connection as quickly as possible • I let go of any negative thoughts, judgments and feelings I have about the situation so we reconnect with trust once more).

c. **(mcs) Non-coherent amends is involved?**
(mcs) {1–6}. *[cr] *(will be on/umb on)*.
1. I don't even recognize when I have made a mistake.
2. I justify and defend my mistakes until I have proved that it was not my mistake and that I am not to blame for the situation.
3. (I cannot say sorry under any circumstance • saying sorry stresses me out).
4. I blame (*name person*) for mistakes I have made.
5. I have to be right.
6. (I make others wrong • I blame (*name person*) for the mistake and go into negative judgments about him/her).

O. **Identify the Five Elements involved with connection to the heart**
(mcs) {1–5} and the item needed.
1. **The Fire Element**
   a. **(mcs) A non-coherent Fire Element quality is firing an old neural pathway?**
   (mcs) {1–6}. *[cr] *(will be on/umb on)*.
   1. I am immature in how I communicate.
   2. I just want to party, have fun and keep my communications on the surface.
   3. I don't feel loved.
   4. I wall myself off from people and then feel alone.
   5. (I am inappropriately open • I make myself vulnerable before love and trust have been established • in my intimate relationships I reveal mistakes or deeper truths prematurely before trust has been established).
   6. (I clam up • I don't know what to talk about).

   b. **(mcs) A coherent Fire Element quality is needed in order to create a new neural pathway of connection in this relationship?**
   (mcs) {1–5}. *[cr] *(will be off/umb off)*.
   1. I bring pleasure, laughter and joy to my communications.

2. I love connecting with people and getting to know them deeply.
3. I build a relationship of trust with (others/*name person*) through our communication.
4. I am interested in others and enjoy enabling others to share (who they are • their interests • what is important to them).
5. I see (*name person's*/other's) strengths and share my positive perceptions.

2. **The Earth Element**
   a. **(mcs) A non-coherent Earth Element quality is firing an old neural pathway?**
      (mcs) {1–6}. *[cr] *(will be on/umb on)*.
      1. (My needs aren't met in relationship • I focus on taking care of others' needs rather than develop a reciprocal relationship).
      2. I feel worried, anxious and overwhelmed when communicating.
      3. I lose my center of equilibrium when communicating.
      4. I try to take care of everything and everyone rather than relax and allow things to happen naturally.
      5. I am only concerned with communicating what I need, and ignore what others may need.
      6. (I can't stop talking • I dominate conversations with my talking).

   b. **(mcs) A coherent Earth Element quality is needed in order to create a new neural pathway of connection in this relationship?**
      (mcs) {1–4}. *[cr] *(will be off/umb off)*.
      1. I handle communication with balance, maintaining my equilibrium when dealing with challenging people and situations.
      2. I am calm, relaxed and centered in the here and now.
      3. Through listening, I am aware of people's needs as well as my own and I am open to each person's needs being met.
      4. I am nurtured when I create a meaningful connection through open communication and reciprocal sharing.

3. **The Metal Element**
   a. **(mcs) A non-coherent Metal Element quality is firing an old neural pathway?**
      (mcs) {1–5}. *[cr] *(will be on/umb on).*
      1. I see *(name person's/*others') failings and point them out.
      2. I put down *(name person/*others).
      3. I cut off from *(name person/*others) when he/she fails to live up to what I believe is important or right.
      4. I don't feel respected and appreciated when we communicate.
      5. I don't respect and appreciate *(name person/*others) in our communications.

   b. **(mcs) A coherent Metal Element quality is needed in order to create a new neural pathway of connection in this relationship?**
      (mcs) {1–7}. *[cr] *(will be off/umb off).*
      1. I feel uplifted and inspired communicating with *(name person/*others).
      2. I bring meaning to *(name person)*'s life through sharing and understanding.
      3. I am authentic in my communications.
      4. I am honest and share my truth.
      5. I value my connection and communication with *(name person/*others).
      6. I know how to express my (opinion • need • ideas) calmly and respectfully so I am heard.
      7. When *(name person/*someone) does something that upsets me, I communicate my feelings and needs rather than (cut off • withdraw from relating with him/her).

4. **The Water Element**
   a. **(mcs) A non-coherent Water Element quality is firing an old neural pathway?**
      (mcs) {1–8}. *[cr] *(will be on/umb on).*
      1. I am afraid to have deeply intimate disclosures with *(name person)*.
      2. Communicating with *(name person/*others) exhausts me.

3. I am afraid to set boundaries on what I perceive as negative behavior by communicating my feelings and needs.
4. I don't listen to (*name person*/ others).
5. I get confused and can't think clearly when communicating with (*name person*/others).
6. I am secretive.
7. I feel that my communications with people (are shallow • never go deeper).
8. I am unable to take a communication to a deeper level of sharing.

b. **(mcs) A coherent Water Element quality is needed in order to create a new neural pathway of connection in this relationship?** (**mcs**) {1–8}. *[**cr**] *(will be off/umb off)*.
   1. I am energized listening deeply to others.
   2. I instinctually know who (*name person*) is, beyond his/her symptoms/problems.
   3. I am calm in the back-and-forth flow of talking, listening and silence.
   4. I listen carefully and respond to what I hear.
   5. I listen and bring clarity to what is going on.
   6. I set boundaries in a loving way rather than with severity, anger or fear.
   7. I have the courage to share myself openly once trust is established.
   8. I share my wisdom in a way that deepens the connection.

5. **The Wood Element**
   a. **(mcs) A non-coherent Wood Element quality is firing an old neural pathway?** (**mcs**) {1–8}. *[**cr**] *(will be on/umb on)*.
      1. I get (frustrated • impatient • angry) in communications.
      2. (I get impatient when (*name person*/other) only talks about themselves and has no interest in what I have to share • I become pessimistic about whether connection is possible).
      3. I am judgmental about (*name person*/others), which comes in the way of having a meaningful relationship.

4. Communicating creates conflict (when decisions need to be made • when (*name person*/others) doesn't take on board what I am sharing).
5. I lose control and start (swearing • using abusive language).
6. I feel hopeless when I am not understood.
7. I react with anger in response to what I perceive as negative behavior in others.

b. **(mcs) A coherent Wood Element quality is needed in order to create a new neural pathway of connection in this relationship? (mcs) {1–7}. *[cr]** *(will be off/umb off).*
1. I love the growth and change that come as a result of sharing thoughts and feelings, and handling differences.
2. I always bring a sense of hope in my communications with (*name person*/ others).
3. I find constructive ways (to communicate what is important to me • to create the positive change that is needed), free of getting angry, defensive, judgmental and reactive.
4. I avoid nagging (*name person*/other) and discuss what is important to me and whether he/she can make it a priority.
5. I avoid talking negatively about (*name person*).
6. I talk about (*name person*) with a friend/coach as a means of gaining a higher perspective.

P. Identify the Energizing Option needed for resonating with communicating for connection in relationship

See SPIRAL UP! book for complete list of all Energizing Options.

a. Another possible Energizing Option is to identify the four birth notes of the client and the person involved with the heart connection problem. Sometimes one of each person's birth notes is the same for both people, and this may be the note that needs to be toned, or used with a Tuning Fork. *See p.25 for the birth note chart and* (**mcs**) *for details.*

b. Resonance Repatterning practitioners will now recheck the *[cr] statements and confirm any change in resonance.

HOW TO USE THE LISTENING TO THE HEART REPATTERNING IN YOUR DAILY LIFE
EVEN IF YOU HAVE NOT YET ATTENDED A RESONANCE REPATTERNING SEMINAR

- Choose one of the ten facets of Heart Connection, do an Energizing Option (from SPIRAL UP!) to resonate with its quality(s), and practice that one facet in all your communications.

- At the end of your day, ask yourself, "What inspired me? What moved me? What surprised me?" If possible journal your answers. Observe the changes once you have done this for several months.

- Do B + C + D + an Energizing Option.

- Do B + O + the Birth note Energizing Option.

RR SESSIONS: *If you would like to receive the complete Repatterning with a professional Resonance Repatterning Practitioner, in person or over the phone, go to ResonanceRepatterning.net > Sessions for RR Institute Practitioners worldwide who have listed themselves on the RRI website.*

RR SEMINARS: *If you would like to attend Resonance Repatterning seminars in person or online, so you can use RR effectively on yourself and/or others, go to ResonanceRepatterning.net > Seminars for the list of teachers endorsed by the Resonance Repatterning Institute to teach.*

3. THE MATURE HEART

My mother-in-law (who just died at the age of 96) didn't leave
the world with any 'works', didn't build anything, didn't win
any prizes. And yet she gave us all the gift of a shining example.
She never said a bad word about anyone, never complained,
never shunned her responsibilities. She just soldiered on, and
did things right. She listened, and understood, and smiled, and
nodded. That alone was a gift.

Kristin Zhivago, *business coach and consultant*

Someone once asked me, "What does it mean to be mature in our relationships?"
I didn't have an immediate answer, but questions require answers, so her question
got me thinking about four different aspects of maturity and immaturity and
how they impact our relationships:

1. As the **Five Elements of Chinese Acupuncture** are a map for understanding
    ourselves, our relationships and our world, I wondered what they could teach
    us about maturity.

2. Our **autonomic nervous system stress responses** have a direct impact on our
    relationships in terms of maturity and immaturity.

3. Another significant way of looking at the theme of maturity is from the point
    of view of **women in relationship to their significant other or husband, and
    men in relation to their significant other or wife** and how this may help us
    create more love in intimate relationship.

4. And then there is a deeper way of looking at **maturity – from a spiritual
    perspective**. Maturity from this point of view is represented by our higher
    mind, which wants self-mastery over the negative tendencies of our own

lower mind: the higher mind being the mature aspect of ourselves and the lower mind the immature aspect.

Maturity and the kid within

Although maturity is essential in our relationships, 'being mature' is not necessarily a state we aspire to. If someone told us as a kid to be mature, it was usually a clamp down on having fun and enjoying ourselves. So maturity is often associated with being grown-up, serious, boring or worse – having to be responsible!

1. **Maturity and the Five Elements of Chinese Acupuncture**

   Fortunately, in terms of the Five Elements of Chinese Acupuncture, joy, laughter and having a sense of fun as well as being responsible for our obligations are all on the same side of the fence. All these qualities are a part of maturity.

   - **The Fire Element and maturity**

     The Fire Element is directly associated with maturing, and also with fun, joy, laughter and how we relate to others.

     The Fire Element correlates with the season of summer where plants grow to their fullest maturity. So in us maturing is related to our capacity for growing to our fullest potential.

     If our Fire Element is weak, we won't mature in this way, we won't achieve our fullest potential of growth. We may be like Peter Pan or Wendy: the eternal child. Lots of fun and laughter, playfulness, having a great time, going to parties, loving to be around people, but also a resistance to growing up.

     Wanting to stay a young plant forever is a lack of maturing.

     Even if we aren't a Peter Pan or Wendy, many of us in our relationships are like small children in our reactiveness: temper tantrums, needy, jealous, argumentative – we too haven't grown up!

Most of us, if we are honest, are scared of the maturing process, which is associated with old age. We want the appearance of staying eternally young: we dye our hair, have facelifts, breast implants, tummy tucks, hair implants, and generously support the multi-billion dollar industry that provides us with face creams and supplements that claim to be the fountain of youth and to erase all the wrinkles our lifestyle has created. Our hope is to keep looking young and gorgeous until we die!

We forget that the Fire energy is within us, not outside us.

When our Fire Element is mature, we automatically become ageless and manifest the strengths of the Fire Element:

- We have joy in life.

- We love to laugh.

- We have fun.

- We love to smile at each person we meet, to connect.

- We don't need to do anything artificial to 'stay' young. We simply *are* youthful and vibrant, even with gray hair!

- We are naturally bright and humorous, have a warm, attractive almost charismatic quality that draws other people into our orbit.

- We grow to our fullest potential – whether an oak tree or a daffodil – in every sphere of our life.

These Fire qualities are within each of us.

- **The Earth Element and maturity**
  When our Earth energy is non-coherent, or we lack maturity in our Earth Element energy, we may try to take care of everything and everyone, often to the point of exhaustion. We lose our center. We are ungrounded.

Earth is about being in our center of balance, poise, equilibrium. We move out into the world to take care of others from a centered place. When we are grounded we also take care of our own needs.

With non-coherent or immature Earth, we pour our time and energy out and out, excessively taking care of others, but ignoring our own needs.

We then become anxious, worried or overwhelmed by the responsibilities we have taken on. We may even feel victimized by our circumstances: upset there is no one to take care of us, resentful that we give but are not getting anything back in return.

At the other extreme, our immature Earth may drive us to be excessively needy – constantly pulling on people to give us attention, to listen endlessly to our worries and problems and no matter how much attention and help we receive, it is never enough.

Non-coherent Earth energy is the side of the fence where being grown up and mature is a burden. It is the part of us that still wants to be free: to play, have fun and be taken care of. The child within is not ready for the adult responsibility of taking care of others. When we resonate with coherent Earth Element qualities, this non-coherence ceases to exist.

When our Earth Element is mature, the strengths of the Earth Element qualities manifest naturally:

- We are able to keep our center of balance and equilibrium in any situation.

- We are generous in our giving, free of any need or desire for a reward.

- We love helping others.

- We are empathetic – genuinely feeling for others' pain and the troubles they are going through.

- We see the needs of others and want to help people meet their needs.

- We are mothering, devoted and love to be of service.

- We harvest riches from all our life experiences – both the good as well as the challenging.

- We receive all the nurturing we need in order to recharge our energies for yet more giving.

- We help others to maintain their center of equilibrium when they are going through troubled times.

- We stand on our own two feet, not leaning too much on others or having others lean too much on us.

- We enjoy being responsible for meeting our own needs and obligations and taking care of others free of feeling over-burdened.

- **The Metal Element and maturity**
Metal is associated with what is valuable – gold, silver and other precious metals.

  If our Metal Element is non-coherent or immature, we won't see brilliance in ourselves or others. We tend to focus on our failures rather than our successes. We may demean ourselves, put ourselves down and judge ourselves.

  Equally, we may judge others, demean others, always seeing others' imperfections and failures, rather than seeing and acknowledging what we appreciate.

  Immature Metal Element energy may cause us to cut off a relationship if we feel disrespected, devalued or if a friend fails to live up to what we value, to what we feel is right. Even with an old friend or the person we are married to we may suddenly cut off without any opening for communication or resolution of the problem.

When we are immature in our Metal Element, we crave respect, appreciation and validation, often fantasizing about winning awards and being famous!

The catch 22 with our immature Metal Element energy is that when we are given the appreciation and respect we long for, we may not accept it because it is not given in exactly the way we want it – in other words, we don't resonate with receiving the respect we want.

When our Metal Element energy is mature, the strengths of the Metal Element manifest naturally:

- We are authentic. We follow our truth, our north star, and walk our talk. Mature Metal always takes the high road.

- We use our brilliant mind to bring clear thinking to any situation.

- We live by high spiritual values.

- We make every decision according to whether it is aligned to our spiritual values and priorities.

- We stay connected to what is most valuable within us, which is our spirit – the essence of who we are – and to the divine in others.

- We value and appreciate ourselves and see what is valuable in others.

- We let go of everything that is unimportant or has no value.

- We value who we are.

- **The Water Element and maturity**
  The Water Element is associated with power and energy. We may not use our willpower to conserve our energy or overcome poor habits that stop positive relationships from growing and deepening.

  With an immature Water Element we may feel powerless, or we may have power but abuse or misuse it.

Equally, we may waste our energy, use it up, and become exhausted and ill. We may use up more energy than we are able to recharge. We don't get enough sleep. We don't energize ourselves by eating nutritious food. We deplete our reserves and are left exhausted and unwell.

Energy is associated with our resources, including money resources. When our Water Element is immature we tend to waste our resources: money pours through our fingers like sand. We get into debt. We spend more than we earn. We max out our credit cards.

Similarly, if we don't recharge our relationships, they also becomes exhausted and unwell.

Because the Water Element is associated with fear, immaturity may stop us from facing life with courage. We may avoid life and relationship because of fear.

Most important, with immature Water energy, we don't use our energy to manifest our life purpose or our spiritual potential.

When our Water Element is mature, the strengths of the Water Element manifest naturally:

- We have all the energy, power, money and resources we need to move through life with courage, drive and ambition.

- Our Water Element energy is like the Niagara Falls: huge power that can be channeled and used for manifesting our life purpose and spiritual potential.

- We have the drive and energy to manifest our intentions and vision.

- We have the willpower and wisdom to conserve our energy, our resources, and to use our resources for overcoming our weaknesses and manifesting our purpose and potential.

- We move forward in life with courage, facing our fears rather than being daunted by them.

- **The Wood Element and maturity**

  When we are immature in our Wood Element, we tend to be judgmental, impatient, easily irritated, frustrated and angry in response to anything that holds us back from what we want, that is too slow or that constrains us. Immature Wood wants what it wants now, no delayed gratification!

  We may lack the assertive energy to manifest our vision. We have great ideas that go nowhere. Or we may be overly assertive in getting what we want.

  We may become frustrated and angry about our present reality, which never matches our vision of what could be. We may even lose sight of our vision of what is possible, stop creating goals, or find ourselves unable to make good decisions about what to do or where to begin. We may slip into becoming hopeless and pessimistic about positive change and growth towards our goals even being possible.

  Immature Wood energy fails to push through obstacles, unlike grass that pushes through cement in its drive to grow towards the light. We give up. We don't attempt to start over when facing failure. We no longer stand up for what is right. We no longer know who we are or strive to attain our potential.

  When our Wood Element is mature, the strengths of the Wood Element manifest naturally:
  - Mature Wood Element energy, associated with the season of spring, leaps into life, filled with hope, vision and the urge for new growth.

  - We know who we are. We have a clear sense of our own identity – whether an oak tree, a cypress or a rose.

  - We respond to the inner urge to keep growing and learning.

  - We have a vision of our potential and our goal – that even if I am a tiny acorn, I know that within me is the huge oak tree and I will grow into that which I am.

- We are able to see our present reality and yet also envision where we are going and what we want to achieve – and make plans for getting there over time.

- We stand for what we believe and are willing to fight for our beliefs.

- We are patient with our own process of growth and that of others. The farmer sows the seed, knowing that the harvest comes later.

Sir Ernest Shackleton is a powerful example of mature Wood energy: he faced his present reality of twenty-seven of his crew stuck on an ice flow for eighteen months in the South Antarctic, freezing cold, little food and no hope of rescue.

At the same time he was able to sustain his vision that his crew would return home alive and safe. Every decision he made was aligned to this vision. No matter what disaster occurred, no matter what mistakes, he remained optimistic and hopeful. Day in and day out he focused on the next action for achieving his goal: saving the lives of his men. And against all odds, he realized his vision.

Only someone with mature Wood Element energy could have overcome the challenges he faced.

2. **Maturity and our autonomic nervous system**
Now let's look at maturity in our close relationships in terms of our nervous system.

One important aspect of our physiology, which we have in common with animals, is the sympathetic branch of our autonomic nervous system. Our SNS reacts instantaneously to stress factors. It is our means of survival.

But powerful as this fight-flight system is, it wreaks havoc with our level of maturity in our close relationships.

If we need to run away from a bear or fight a tiger, OK, like animals we do what we have to do to save ourselves.

But what about all the times we go into a fight-flight survival response with the person we're married to, or with our children or our friends and colleagues, as though they were a bear or a tiger?

We react as though our survival is at stake. The intense fear we experience (a flight response) or the irritation and anger as we blow our top (a fight response) are animal survival reactions, rather than human responses.

Maturity and positive relationships are only possible when we transcend our SNS fight-flight responses and activate our thinking/feeling brain-heart to discern what is truly life threatening in our relationships and what isn't.

Being human

Human responses are very different from fight-flight reactive SNS responses. Human responses are activated by our higher-brain centers and are motivated by empathy and love.

For instance, there was the plane that had trouble gaining height because of ice on its wings. It landed in the Potomac river in the middle of a Washington D.C. winter. People jumped into the freezing water to help the survivors who had managed to climb out of the back of the plane.

This is a human response, not a survival reaction. And one survivor, who managed to climb out of the plane himself, stayed to help others out: people on the bank saw his hand pushing others to the surface of the river, until finally his hand disappeared.

This is the human spirit in action that serves out of love and wants what is best for others.

We could say that true maturity is when the human spirit transcends our animal survival system.

Ultimate maturity is when love is our primary response and we meet all challenging situations with inner strength, coming from the power of a loving response.

Fight-flight reactiveness blocks our awareness of this love and our ability to respond with love even when we may need to be firm or stern.

Maturity versus fight-flight in relationship
In most marriages we tend to live in sympathetic nervous system (SNS) fight-flight reactions rather than respond from a spirit of love. A spiritual adept in India once told a friend, "If you knew what anger did to your body, you would never get angry again for any reason."

Destructive reactions, or submitting to destructive behaviors, are symptoms of distress. They require healing of past pains and resolution of past traumas that continue to be superimposed on the present.

When mature, we know that we have one or two seconds to access our higher brain centers before the SNS activates a stress adrenaline-cortisol reactive response. Once the instantaneous fight-flight reaction is activated, there is no enzyme that can stop it. **It takes up to six hours for the adrenal-cortisol fight-flight response to return to normal.**

Mostly we go into these inappropriate survival reactions when some need is not met. Looking at needs, expressing our needs and making sure that our needs are met is important – and is a sign of maturity.

3. **Maturity and women in relation to men**
There is an interesting little book by Shaunti Feldhahn called *For Women Only: what you need to know about the inner lives of men*.

Shaunti did a survey of men of all ages to find out what was truly important to them in relation to their wives. It is fascinating looking at what she discovered and we will analyze it in relation to the Five Elements of Chinese Acupuncture and the theme of maturity.

The importance of the Metal Element for men

Nearly all women want to receive unconditional love with lots of affection – touch, talking, listening, head nodding and eye contact.

However, Shaunti discovered that what men want most is **unconditional respect.** Seventy-four percent of the men in the survey said they would rather feel unloved than inadequate or disrespected.

The men in the survey said they wanted their wife to respect their knowledge, their opinions and their decisions. And they wished their wives wouldn't argue with their decisions all the time!

In particular the men said they wanted their wife to stand by them in public, even when they might not deserve it.

When a woman criticizes her man in public (or behind his back) or jokes about a weakness he may have, he feels devastated and humiliated: he loses his self-confidence, feels inadequate and what is worse he feels that he loses the respect of other men and his colleagues.

Men need their wives to build them up in public: ask his opinion, appreciate something he did well. For a man this is the equivalent of him bringing his wife a bunch of roses and giving her all the appreciation, affection and unconditional love she yearns for!

Almost 72% of the men, in spite of looking or being competent, said they feel insecure about others' opinions of them and their abilities and have a fear of criticism and judgments.

If a woman feels insecure, she talks with her women friends or asks for help. Not so for men, who need to feel and be competent and successful at what they do without asking for help.

What is particularly sad is that 52% of the men felt unappreciated at home. Instead of coming home and feeling validated, the same battle continues at home: competition, disagreements and a lack of acknowledgment.

Perhaps what is most important for women to hear is that men judge themselves based on the happiness of their wives and the respect their wives have for them.

In a conflict with their partner, 81% of the men felt their wife or significant other didn't respect them. But when affirmed by their wife – that she believes he can do anything – this gives the man the confidence to conquer the world.

Also to do with Metal maturity: men really like it when their wife takes care of her appearance. She doesn't have to be perfect, but he appreciates her efforts to keep herself in good shape and dress nicely. Her self-respect supports his sense of value and validation by others – particularly by other men.

The importance of the Earth Element for men

Shaunti also discovered in her survey that the biggest responsibility a man feels, most if not all the time, is to be the family provider – even if his wife earns a living.

The man wants to know that he can provide for his family and he wants his wife's appreciation for his hard work, even when he works long hours and is away from home.

Many women complain about their husband's long work hours, not understanding that their man wants to provide for them and that he lives in fear that he may not be able to create material security for his family.

The importance of the Wood Element for men

When a woman nags at her partner – a form of anger – he hears it as distrust of him: that he is lazy, a failure, and that she is disappointed in him.

Wood is about plans and decisions, having a list of goals or priorities and going into action to achieve them. From a man's point of view, his not doing what she wants when she wants it may simply be that what she wants is not as high on his list of priorities as it is on hers!

The importance of the Fire Element for men
Sexuality and intimacy are associated with the Fire Element.

For most women, Fire Element qualities of feeling loved and loving is mostly through appreciation, affection, eye contact, loving touch and listening. For most men, feeling loved and loving often occurs through sexual connection.

When a man's desire for sexual connection is turned down by his partner, most men feel rejected and cut off in the same way a woman would feel if her husband gave her the silent treatment and refused to communicate with her or give her affection.

In a mature relationship, both needs are satisfied: the couple harmoniously communicate their individual needs in terms of sexual bonding and non-sexual affection.

The importance of the Water Element for men
The Water Element is about power and the energy to move forward.

What most women do not realize and something Shaunti discovered – is that a man's power comes from their wife!

The four most important things
When Shaunti asked the men to say four things they wanted their wives to know, something they wanted to communicate to them about what was most important, they said:
- "I want her to know how much I love her."

- Of second importance to men was that his partner make more of an effort to take care of herself in how she looks and dresses.

- Of third importance: "I need more respect in private and in public."

- And tying for fourth place was, "I need more sex" and "I need her to understand my burden to provide and how draining my job is."

4. **Maturity from a spiritual perspective**

Spiritual maturity is about being responsible for our own right actions and accepting that others are responsible for their own actions.

Spiritual maturity is also about going beyond our negative tendencies, habits or addictions. Each one of us is challenged to have self-mastery over our own weaknesses, rather than focusing on the faults of others and the negative tendencies **they** need to overcome!

At the core, whether a man or woman, there are a few basic human needs: We all want to love and be loved. We all need to be appreciated for the little daily things we do. We want to feel at home and relaxed with others. We long for acceptance, free of all judgments. And we need to share ourselves: to be heard as well as to hear others share themselves and be heard.

There is a constant push-pull between succumbing to the desires of our lower mind need for immediate gratification and pleasure (and our SNS stress response when these desires are not met), and the urge to express the positive qualities of our higher mind and spirit. A wonderful story illustrates this mind-spirit conflicting predicament.

GETTING THE DONKEY TO CROSS THE STREAM

Once upon a time a man was trying to get his donkey to cross a stream. The donkey stood on the bank and refused to budge. The man shouted, pushed and pulled and still the donkey wouldn't move.

Finally a friend suggested, "Why not give your donkey love, then he'll easily be led across the stream." So the man tried giving his donkey love, but the obstinate animal still refused to move.

Frustrated and angry the man turned to his friend and said, "All right, let's see *you* get the donkey to cross the stream with love."

The friend took a 2 x 4 plank of wood, hit the donkey over the head with it and then lovingly led the donkey across the stream.

The man was shocked, "You call that *love*?" The friend replied, "Well, first I had to get its attention!"

If doing the Repatterning, return to {G a} p.103

∾

Meaning in relation to maturity

Crossing the stream represents growth, change, self-mastery, manifesting our spiritual potential and our purpose in life. It is about realizing a higher state of consciousness, of positivity. In other words, maturity and what it means to be human.

The donkey represents the mind's lower tendencies. It is the animal part of us – the aspect of us that resists improving ourself and being open to positive change and growth. The donkey is the ego-part of us that wants to be right, that won't listen, that won't let go of old ways of being that no longer serve us: the grudges, upsets, problems, traumas, pain, sickness. The obstinate donkey within holds on to suffering rather than move forward into positive change.

The owner of the donkey represents the mind's higher tendencies. This aspect of us wants change, growth and a higher state of consciousness. Our higher mind tries every tactic and strategy to improve – but with no results because donkey and man must cross this stream together. Our lower mind must become aligned to spiritual principles if we want to realize a higher state of consciousness.

Sometimes our donkey mind takes a few steps forward with our higher mind. Other times our donkey mind refuses to go further. Sometimes we are mature – living a principled life. And sometimes we are immature – we do and say things we are not proud of.

The friend represents the sage, the spiritual teacher. The teacher whacks our donkey lower mind over the head. The teacher gets our attention. As long as our attention is turned outward into the world towards lower tendencies, we won't realize our spiritual potential within. Once our attention turns inward and upward, we are easily and lovingly guided across the stream of life towards higher consciousness.

We learn everything through the grace of our teachers, whether learning to read and write, the sciences, the arts or spirituality. The greater the teacher, along with the efforts of the student (we do have to walk across the stream), the more easily we are guided towards realizing our spiritual potential as mature human beings.

So maturity keeps us focused on what is most important for our spiritual growth and how our relationships are an opportunity for our own personal transformation.

Summary

We have looked at our Five Elements in relation to maturity, our fight-flight SNS responses and maturity, Shaunti Feldhan's survey of what men want that could support maturity in close relationship and finally maturity from a spiritual perspective.

The MATURITY IN RELATIONSHIP REPATTERNING that follows looks at some of these issues associated with maturity so we resonate with a new awareness of how we can enhance our relationships and our life.

Resonance Repatterning helps us strengthen the first three aspects (our Five Elements, SNS responses and the needs of women and men) so we resonate with more balanced responses. But to bring these strengths into our everyday relationships takes something more: Action! Practice!

And then for spiritual maturity we need to be receptive to the Friend, the spiritual teacher, who is always ready to get our attention and guide us towards expanded consciousness and love.

FURTHER READING

Bach Flower Essences for the Family. Oxfordshire.

Philip M. Chancellor. *Handbook of the Bach Flower Remedies*.

Shaunti Feldhahn. *For Women Only: What you need to know about the inner lives of men*.

3. MATURE HEART REPATTERNING

A. **Name the problem in your close relationship**
Do {a-d} in sequence.

a. *Ask*, "What is the problem you want to resolve in your relationship(s)?" *[**cr**] (*will be on/umb on because client resonates with the out-of-sync frequencies causing this problem*).

b. *Ask*, "How do you feel (*name person*) is immature?" *[**cr**] (*will be on/ umb on because client resonates with the perception that (name person) is immature in the situation*).

c. *Ask*, "How do you respond negatively to (*name person*)'s (*immature quality*)?" *[**cr**] (*will be on/umb on because client resonates with this reactive immature reaction*).

d. *Ask,* "How are you immature in your relationship with (*name person*)?" *[**cr**] (*will be on/umb on*).

B. **Identify the underlying need that was not met in the past that client needs to resonate with in the present in order to create maturity in relationship**

1. **The need for security and survival**
   (**mcs**) {1–9}.
   1. (I am cared for • I am looked after • My needs are met).
   2. I feel secure.
   3. Everything is provided for.
   4. (I survive • I am successful).
   5. I am protected.
   6. I have a home.
   7. I am clothed, fed and kept warm.
   8. (I am welcomed • I belong).
   9. Other: *Ask,* "What do you need in order to feel secure about your survival?"

2. **Physical needs for health and energy**
   (**mcs**) {1–10}.
   1. I take in and appreciate living food (mother's milk • fresh homegrown fruits and vegetables • pure water).
   2. I breathe pure air.
   3. (I am warm • I receive the warmth of the sun).
   4. (I move for life • I am energized by movement).
   5. I sleep well and wake up refreshed.
   6. I receive all the (sunlight • full-spectrum light) I need.
   7. I do those actions that lead to health and energy.
   8. I think positive thoughts and feel good about myself and others.
   9. I relax and rejuvenate myself.
   10. Other: *Ask,* "What do you need for your health and energy?"

3. **The need to achieve your best, go beyond your limits and manifest your potential**
   (**mcs**) {1–12}.
   1. (I achieve my best • I value those who help me achieve my best).
   2. (I manifest my potential • I am successful • I enjoy going beyond the limits of what I thought was possible).
   3. I have the strength and faith to persevere through obstacles and apparent failures.
   4. I serve (others • humanity).
   5. I play (joyfully • spontaneously).
   6. I am curious.
   7. (I create beauty • I am creative in everything I do).
   8. I am confident.
   9. I am courageous.
   10. I maintain an optimistic attitude no matter what difficulties I'm facing.
   11. I put my concern for human well-being and right action before my need for (material success • the achievement of my ambitions).
   12. Other: *Ask,* "What do you need that would allow you to manifest your potential, go beyond the limits of what you think is possible and achieve your best?"

4. **The need for love and respect in relationship**
   (**mcs**) {1–19}.
   1. I (receive love • give love • feel worthy of being loved) in my relationship with (*name person*).
   2. I have (close • affectionate • caring) relationships.
   3. I belong and feel (welcomed • included • wanted).
   4. I am enough.
   5. I make loving connections through warm and relaxed eye contact.
   6. I give and receive loving touch.
   7. I am protected from harm.
   8. I have clear safe boundaries • I feel safe.
   9. I am (appreciated • acknowledged • valued • respected • accepted).
   10. I enjoy harmonious relationships.
   11. (I have positive communication in my relationship(s) • I am heard • I hear).
   12. (I am seen • I see).
   13. I freely express my (truth • feelings • thoughts • ideas • humor).
   14. I (relax and laugh • enjoy humor).
   15. I am free to explore and return for loving touch and bonding whenever I need to.
   16. My heart is open to (compassion • understanding • love).
   17. (I forgive • I am forgiven • I resolve problems and grow in my capacity to love).
   18. I let go of (reactiveness • blame • complaints • feeling a victim • gossip).
   19. Other: *Ask,* "What do you need that would bring you love and respect in your relationship(s)?"

5. **The need for meaning, purpose, love, and happiness from within**
   (**mcs**) {1–20}.
   1. (I feel joyful • I let go of all negative thoughts and tune in to love).
   2. I am filled with gratitude every day.
   3. (I see beauty • I see the Divine) in every aspect of the creation.
   4. I am content.
   5. (I have faith • I trust that every experience is for my highest good).

6. I am (focused • disciplined).
7. (I pay attention to my thoughts and the stillness of my mind • I am still).
8. I accept the divine will, free of resistance and fear.
9. I live my (truth • values) in action.
10. I love unconditionally.
11. (I stand for what is right • I live with integrity).
12. (I practice the presence of God • I feel spiritually connected at all times to the Divine within).
13. I let go of (self-importance • negative thoughts and feelings).
14. (I am at peace • My mind is peaceful).
15. (I am receptive to divine grace).
16. (I serve selflessly • I give generously • I find every opportunity to help others).
17. I stay conscious of the light within and the light within each person I meet.
18. I am receptive to the higher purpose and meaning of every circumstance life brings.
19. I let go of my need to get (upset • angry) about anything in this world.
20. Other: *Ask,* "What do you need for your spiritual well-being?"

C. **(mcs) We need to identify the chronic Sympathetic Nervous System (SNS) stress response being activated and causing the lack of maturity and love in the relationship?**
   (**mcs**) Client needs to hear anything from maturity versus fight/flight in relationship? *p.83*

   (**mcs**) {1–3} for the SNS stress response being activated.
   1. **The alert response**
      a. (**mcs**) We need to identify the past non-coherent alert neural pathway being reactivated in the present situation that client still resonates with?
         (**mcs**) {1–7}. *[**cr**] *(will be on/umb on).*

1. I (freeze • am incapable of action • am paralyzed).
2. I am inappropriately triggered into a hyper-aroused state.
3. I (hide • isolate myself) because life is so dangerous.
4. I am startled by (small things • anything).
5. I can't relax because I can't (see who or what is dangerous • locate the source of a danger).
6. I am on the alert for danger all the time.
7. I am tense all the time.

b. (mcs) We need to identify the coherent alert response client needs to resonate with in order to create a new neural pathway of maturity and love in the present relationship?
(mcs) {1–12}. *[cr] *(will be off/umb off)*.
   1. I am alert and ready for action.
   2. I am alert yet relaxed.
   3. I orient myself away from danger.
   4. I orient myself towards what is nourishing, bonding and supports my survival.
   5. I am curious.
   6. If no threat is present I immediately relax.
   7. I quickly locate where there is danger and who is involved.
   8. I am confident.
   9. I am able to identify and meet any challenge.
   10. I access a wide range of options and reactions.
   11. If there is no threat I release residual activated energy by moving, trembling or shaking out.
   12. I easily move through states of tense hyper-vigilance and relaxed alertness.

2. **The fight response**
   a. (mcs) We need to identify the past non-coherent fight neural pathway client still resonates with?
   (mcs) {1–12}. *[cr] *(will be on/umb on)*.
      1. (I am defensive • I overreact).
      2. I am overly assertive.

3. (I am quarrelsome • I pick quarrels).
4. I am (impatient • angry • frustrated • enraged).
5. I easily become violent.
6. I am hyper-nervous.
7. I am a caretaker for everyone.
8. I am (over-controlling • dominating).
9. (I am excessively talkative • I interrupt (*name person*) before he/she has finished talking).
10. (I make others wrong • I tell (*name person*) that he/she is wrong).
11. I use sex to discharge my anger.
12. I can't keep still.

b. (**mcs**) We need to identify the coherent fight response client needs to resonate with in order to create a new neural pathway of maturity and love in the present relationship?
(**mcs**) {1–5}. *[**cr**] *(will be off/umb off)*.
1. I (defend myself appropriately • set clear boundaries with (clarity • strength • confidence • love).
2. I stand on my own two feet.
3. I am ready to face any challenge with (clarity • focused attention • appropriate decision-making • excitement • the ability to see all sides of the situation).
4. After meeting a challenge I dissipate any residual, mobilized energy by (shaking • trembling • moving • walking • dancing).
5. I share my success in handling a challenge with (*name person*) and relax into love-bonding once more.

3. **The flight response**
a. (**mcs**) We need to identify the past non-coherent flight neural pathway client still resonates with? (**mcs**) {1–9}. *[**cr**] *(will be on/umb on)*.
1. (I am unable to avoid dangerous situations • I habitually put myself in dangerous situations).
2. I run away from situations in a panic, unable to think clearly.
3. (I get in a panic • I am chronically anxious).

4. I turn to (food • alcohol • drugs • cigarettes • sex • sleep • day-dreaming • gambling • other) as a way to escape.
5. (I become ill as a way to avoid a threatening situation • I run away from life).
6. I stop (hearing • seeing • tasting • smelling • feeling).
7. I escape by being depressed.
8. (I can't get going • I can't move into action • I can't (run away • avoid danger).
9. I cry as a way of handling any emotionally-charged situation I can't cope with.

b. (mcs) We need to identify the coherent flight response client needs to resonate with in order to create a new neural pathway of maturity and love in the present relationship? (mcs) {1–4}. *[cr] *(will be off/ umb off)*.
1. I move away from dangerous situations.
2. I am clear and oriented when facing a danger so I know the best way to handle the difficulty.
3. After successfully avoiding a threat I (shake • tremble • move) in order to dissipate any residual mobilized energy.
4. After successfully avoiding a threat, I discharge excess mobilized energy by playing out different ways of successfully escaping and I share my success with (others).

D. (mcs) Client needs to hear anything from the Element introductions?

(mcs) {1–5} for the one needed and read the Element strengths and weaknesses.
1. The Fire Element *p.74*
2. The Earth Element *p.137*
3. The Metal Element *p.77*
4. The Water Element *p.78*
5. The Wood Element *p.80*

Ask, "What weakness and strength do you see in your (*name 1–5 Element*). *[cr] with "My heart matures each time I transform my weakness of (*name weakness*) into the strength to (*name strength*)" *(will be off/umb off).*

E. Identify the Five Elements involved
(**mcs**) {1–5} for the primary one needed.

1. The Fire Element
  a. (**mcs**) **A non-coherent Fire Element quality is firing old neural pathways?** (**mcs**) {1–7}. *[cr] *(will be on/umb on).*
  1. (I want to stay the eternal child • I refuse to grow up).
  2. I just want to party and have fun.
  3. I don't feel loved.
  4. (I feel rejected by my partner when she/he doesn't want to have sex with me when I want it • I don't feel safe having sex with my partner).
  5. I feel over the hill and terrified of growing old.
  6. I wall myself off from people and then feel alone.
  7. I do whatever I need to do to artificially keep looking youthful.

  b. (**mcs**) **A coherent Fire Element quality is needed in order to create new neural pathways of maturity and love in this relationship?** (**mcs**) {1–7}. *[cr] *(will be off/umb off).*
  1. My partner loves me.
  2. I trust my partner.
  3. I understand that my partner's need for sexual connection is an act of love – a way to give love and receive love.
  4. I am ageless and spontaneously joyful in all I do.
  5. I enjoy maturing to my fullest potential and also having joy, fun and laughter in my life.
  6. I attract people through my natural warmth, friendliness and loving interest.
  7. I set boundaries with warmth, humor and love.

2. **The Earth Element**
    a. **(mcs) A non-coherent Earth Element quality is firing old neural pathways? (mcs) {1–7}. *[cr]** *(will be on/umb on).*
        1. My needs aren't met.
        2. I am a victim of circumstances.
        3. I feel worried, anxious and overwhelmed.
        4. I lose my center of equilibrium even in the face of the smallest stress.
        5. I try to take care of everything and everyone and then (go into overwhelm • feel exhausted • feel resentful that I am not receiving anything back).
        6. I am only concerned with what I need, and I want my needs met right now.
        7. I keep giving and giving until I have nothing left to give.

    b. **(mcs) A coherent Earth Element quality is needed in order to create new neural pathways of maturity and love in this relationship? (mcs) {1–6}. *[cr]** *(will be off/umb off).*
        1. I handle life's stresses with balance, maintaining my equilibrium when dealing with challenging people and situations.
        2. I am calm and centered in the here and now.
        3. I am aware of people's needs and support those needs being met.
        4. I am generous in my giving and I also take care of receiving the nurturing I need so I can keep giving more.
        5. I am grounded, standing on my own two feet, and I am able to ask for help when I need it.
        6. I accept (what is • the present situation as it is) and I go into positive action to create a nurturing environment for all.

3. **The Metal Element**
    a. **(mcs) A non-coherent Metal Element quality is firing old neural pathways? (mcs) {1–5}. *[cr]** *(will be on/umb on).*
        1. I see (others' • *name person's*/my partner's) failings and point them out.

2. I put (*name person*/my partner • others) down.
3. I cut off from (*name person*/partner • other) when he/she fails to live up to what I believe is right.
4. I don't feel respected and appreciated.
5. I don't respect and appreciate (*name person*/partner • other)

   b. **(mcs) A coherent Metal Element quality is needed in order to create new neural pathways of maturity and love in this relationship?** (mcs) {1–8}. *[cr] *(will be off/umb off).*
   1. I take care of myself, my health and my appearance.
   2. I respect (*name person*/my partner) in private and in public.
   3. I appreciate and respect (*name person*/my partner) for working hard to support the family.
   4. (I live my authentic truth • I stay aligned with my values of what is most important and true for me • I take the high road in every challenging situation).
   5. I focus on my successes and (*name person's*/ my partner's) successes.
   6. I respect (*name person's*/ my partner's) ideas and opinions, even if they are different from my own.
   7. I respect (*name person*/my partner) for who he/she is and what he/she contributes to my life.
   8. I am respected and valued for who I am and what I contribute.

4. **The Water Element**
   a. **(mcs) A non-coherent Water Element quality is firing old neural pathways?** (mcs) {1–9}. *[cr] *(will be on/umb on).*
   1. I am afraid to be deeply intimate with (*name person*/my partner).
   2. I am exhausted without any reserves of energy.
   3. I am afraid to move forward into action.
   4. I feel powerless to improve my life.
   5. I lack drive and ambition.
   6. I am afraid to set boundaries on what I perceive is negative behavior.

7. I don't listen.
8. I get confused and can't think clearly.
9. I (abuse • misuse) my power.

b. (mcs) A coherent Water Element quality is needed in order to create new neural pathways of maturity and love in this relationship? (mcs) {1–9}. *[cr] (will be off/umb off).
   1. I am ready to go!
   2. I feel energized and powerful.
   3. I am calm even in an emergency.
   4. I listen carefully and respond to what I hear.
   5. I listen and bring clarity to what is going on.
   6. I set boundaries in a loving way rather than with excess energy or fear.
   7. I maintain good reserves of (energy • money).
   8. I channel my energy for realizing the purpose of my life and my potential as a human being.
   9. I recharge my energy reserves through (healthy eating habits • getting sufficient sleep • being out in sunlight every day • drinking enough water).

5. **The Wood Element**
   a. (mcs) A non-coherent Wood Element quality is firing old neural pathways? (mcs) {1–8}. *[cr] (will be on/umb on).
      1. I get frustrated and angry about my present reality.
      2. I become pessimistic about whether positive change is possible.
      3. (I lose sight of my goals • I don't have any goals).
      4. I can't decide what to do.
      5. I lose control and start swearing.
      6. I feel hopeless.
      7. I react with irritation/anger in response to what I perceive as negative behavior in others.
      8. I go into (blame • criticism • negative judgments) in response to (*name person*) not doing what I want.

b. (mcs) A coherent Wood Element quality is needed in order
to create new neural pathways of maturity and love in this
relationship? (mcs) {1–9}. *[cr] *(will be off/umb off)*.
1. I focus on all that is good in (*name person*) and our relationship
and dilute what makes me angry with him/her.
2. I love growing and learning.
3. I grow towards realizing my potential.
4. I am realistic about my present reality and also have a clear vision
of where I want to be and how I will get there.
5. I make plans and decisions that support my bigger vision.
6. I know the damaging effects of my anger and I find constructive
ways to communicate what is important to me and what I need in
order to create the positive change.
7. I avoid nagging (*name person*/my partner) and discuss what is
important to me and whether he/she can put it higher on his/her
list of priorities.
8. I know what I disagree with (*name person*) about, and when and
how to express myself so I am heard.
9. I avoid talking ill of (*name person*) (in public • behind his/her
back • in his/her presence).

F. Five important things in relationship
a. (mcs) Client needs to hear anything from "What men want":
(Metal *p.84*, Earth *p.85*, Wood *p.85*, Fire *p.85*, Water *p.86*)

Ask, "As a man/woman, what positive thing did you learn from hearing
this that would help you in your relationship(s)?" *[cr] *(will be off/
umb off)*.

b. (mcs) {1–4} for what both men and women need in relationship.
*[cr] *(will be off/umb off)*.
1. I let (*name person*) know how much I love him/her.

2. (I take care of myself • I look my best • I stay fit • (*Name person*) appreciates that I take care of myself • When going out (*name person*) enjoys how I look • I enjoy how I look).

3. (I am respectful of my (husband/wife • child • family members) both in private and public • We respect our relationship by being faithful and committed).

4. (I enjoy bonding sexually with my husband/wife/partner and I understand if he/she is not in the mood • We work out our sexual differences with love and respect • I give and receive both sexual bonding along with affectionate touch bonding).

5. We share the responsibilities with children, the family and home.

G. Maturity from a spiritual perspective

Do {a–d} in sequence.

a. Read the story of the donkey *p.87*
Ask, "What positive thing did you learn from this story?" *[cr] *(will be off/umb off)*.

b. (mcs) We need to identify the non-coherent spiritual perspective involved?
(**mcs**) {1–9}. *[cr] *(will be on/umb on)*.

1. I resist positive change.

2. I don't do what is in my highest interest, which is to (*name the highest interest*).

3. I refuse to improve myself.

4. I hold on to old ways of being and acting that don't serve me spiritually.

5. I hold on to suffering.

6. I refuse to listen to my conscience, which tells me what is right.

7. I ignore my higher mind and keep doing actions that pull me down.

8. My attention is down and out into the world of desires and self-indulgence.

9. I don't forgive and forget

c. (**mcs**) We need to identify the coherent spiritual perspective client
    needs to resonate with?
    (**mcs**) {1–7}. *[**cr**] *(will be off/umb off)*.
    1. I embrace (growth • positive change • self-mastery over my lower
        mind tendencies).
    2. I want to realize a higher state of consciousness and go into action
        aligned with my vision.
    3. I let go of (grudges • upsets • problems • traumas • pain • sickness).
    4. I have the will power to act on what my conscience tells me is right.
    5. (I follow (the high road • my higher mind tendencies) • Identify the
        action needed for creating maturity in the present relationship).
    6. I am aligned with my spiritual principles.
    7. I hold my attention inward and upward toward the Divine.

d. **Maturity in action**
    Ask, "What action do you need to take to create maturity in your
    relationship?" *[**cr**] *(will be off/umb off)*.

H. Identify the birth note Energizing Option needed to create heart maturity

a. *See p.25* for client's four birth notes and the four birth notes of the
    person involved. If one of the client's four notes coincides with one of the
    notes of the person involved, this may be the note that is needed.

    (**mcs**) for details:
    •   on the vowel sound needed,

    •   the chakra center needed

    •   whether the note needs to be toned, heard with a tuning fork or the
        tuning fork needs to be held over the chakra center.

b. Resonance Repatterning practitioners will now recheck the *[**cr**]
    statements and confirm any change in resonance.

HOW TO USE THE MATURITY IN RELATIONSHIP REPATTERNING IN YOUR DAILY LIFE
EVEN IF YOU HAVE NOT YET ATTENDED A RESONANCE REPATTERNING SEMINAR

- Whenever you are about to go into a reaction, take a TWO SECOND PAUSE. Be aware that when you refuse to indulge your immediate reactions, which are based on past experiences, those neural pathways begin to atrophy from lack of use. If needed, do an Energizing Option to consciously create new neural pathways for a higher mind response.

- When angry or feeling reactive about someone, take time out to think about everything you like about him/her, everything that is positive about him/her. Turn the person from an enemy into a friend.

- Every time you go into a reaction that you know is not appropriately mature, do something from the Maturity in Relationship Repatterning: (A) identify the Element energy involved, (B) identify the alert, fight, flight SNS response Or do (F) the four important things or (G) maturity from the spiritual perspective. Then do an Energizing Option from SPIRAL UP!

RR SESSIONS: *If you would like to receive the complete Repatterning with a professional Resonance Repatterning Practitioner, in person or over the phone, go to ResonanceRepatterning.net > Sessions for RR Institute Practitioners worldwide who have listed themselves on the RRI website.*

RR SEMINARS: *If you would like to attend Resonance Repatterning seminars in person or online, so you can use RR effectively on yourself and/or others, go to ResonanceRepatterning.net > Seminars for the list of teachers endorsed by the Resonance Repatterning Institute to teach.*

4. DISCONNECT FROM THE HEART –
TRIGGER REACTIONS AND STRESS

In proportion to our body mass, our brain is three times
as large as that of our nearest relatives. This huge organ is
dangerous and painful to give birth to, expensive to build, and,
in a resting human, uses about twenty percent of the body's
energy even though it is just two percent of the body's weight.
There must be some reason for all this evolutionary expense.

Susan Blakemore, quoted by Joe Dispenza,
Evolve Your Brain: The Science of Changing Your Mind

Why we focus on the brain in terms of disconnect from the heart
Our heart, with its own neural brain cells, sends its messages directly to the brain
and body. We cannot separate our heart and our brain.

Stress reactions may push the heart to the point of a heart attack and death.
Equally, stress reactions may cause a stroke or "brain attack" and death.

We know that stress is the major cause of all disease, upset and conflicts.
Stress and our trigger reactions in response to stress can prevent us from living
consciously and connectedly. The first step is to become clear about:

- what these stress trigger reactions are

- where they come from

- why they are so difficult to control

- how they are dangerous for our health

- what opportunity they offer us to develop our higher brain-heart potential

- how to develop new ways for responding to immediate stress, which will support our health, well-being and effectiveness

- how we can maintain our peace of mind in challenging situations, using twelve actions for developing our higher brain options

- how Resonance Repatterning makes it possible for us to resonate with harmonious frequencies so we move beyond unconscious ways of reacting

Heart and brain instantaneous response

When we feel threatened for any reason, we immediately go into a stress response, known as the fight-flight survival response. This emergency response has worked well for millions of years – helping us survive untold hardships and challenges. But what happens when it doesn't work well for us?

Belief about reality or the reality itself are the same for our brain-heart

When we believe or imagine we are threatened, or we are threatened in reality, the physiological response in both situations is exactly the same: our fight-flight sympathetic nervous system (SNS) is triggered, bio-chemical responses are activated and within seconds adrenaline and cortisol flood our bloodstream. In spite of our higher brain centers and powers of reasoning and intelligence, our unconscious stress response takes over, we go into action, and we say or do things that later we wish we could take back!

The result of being taken over by our stress response

- Our heart rate increases

- Shallow speeded-up chest breathing takes over and our blood pressure goes up

- Blood flow moves from our digestive system and our brain to our leg and arm muscles in preparation for a run or fight response

- Hormones that activate our energy are released

- Sugars in our bloodstream are increased so we have all the energy we need to run or fight

- The pupils of our eyes dilate so we can see more clearly

- The brain becomes super aware

And all this because we are stuck in a traffic jam and will be ten minutes late for work! Or the traffic light is green and the car in front of us hasn't moved, and we find ourselves shouting at a driver who can't even hear us. Or we are convinced our partner/friend/boss is wrong and we want him/her to agree that we are right.

We pay a high price for all our stress reactions – justified or not.

The responses that are going on in our brain

We are so habituated to our stress reactions that we are hardly aware they are stress responses. We take them for granted, little knowing the havoc they are playing in our brain, heart and body.

But we need to know what these trigger reactions are doing, otherwise there is no incentive to change them. If we want to enjoy our life free of stress so we can take pleasure in handling our challenges, it helps to understand what happens when we submit to our stress responses.

The limbic midbrain

The limbic brain is where the autonomic nervous system originates, which unconsciously and instantaneously responds to perceived threats even before our conscious mind is aware that something threatening is happening.

Stress responses begin in the limbic or midbrain, which is the major **fear-generating region of our brain**. The limbic brain creates the fear that gets us to run away from a danger.

The amygdala response

The amygdala, which is also a part of the limbic brain, **generates emotions** like rage and aggression so we are ready to fight for our life. The priority of the body-brain system is defense – even if in response to someone on the freeway who harmlessly cuts in front of us!

The hypothalamus response

The hypothalamus, another structure in the limbic brain, immediately manufactures **the chemicals that allow us to feel the way we are thinking**. If we believe or think the driver cutting in front of us could have caused an accident, even if this isn't true, our hypothalamus creates bio-chemical feeling responses of fear or anger, and before we know it we are shouting "You stupid idiot" or worse.

The hippocampus response

Now the hippocampus, a structure that's also located in the apricot-sized limbic brain, joins in. The hippocampus is involved in **creating short and long-term memories by association**. This means that any situation in the present that reminds us of an earlier stress will instantaneously re-activate the same fight-flight adrenaline responses from the past.

This is why our past is always present – influencing us as much today as it did all those years ago. And why it is important to change our resonance with past events that the infant or small child perceived as threatening.

Past and present

In response to our thoughts about a present situation that to our brain looks similar to earlier stressful experiences, our brain fires the neural circuits that cause us to go into the same habitual reactive, angry, blaming or fearful behaviors.

What is worse is that every time we *think* of a present or past stress, these repetitive negative thoughts – firing the same neural circuits with their stress feelings and biochemical responses – reinforce stress neural circuits until they become hardwired in our brain. On automatic pilot, we are unaware that we are controlled by all our unconscious triggers, disconnected from higher-brain clear thinking, heart understanding and conscious choice.

No wonder we feel so out of control.

As a result, living too often becomes a survival response to perceived or real stress situations, rather than our challenges providing an opportunity for us to evolve towards our human and spiritual potential.

Adrenaline and cortisol – do they support life or illness

Our adrenals receive stress messages from our brain-heart. We need to remember that our heart, like our brain, has neurons – what used to be called "brain cells" because they were thought to exist only in the brain. The heart is so significant that in the womb it starts to beat before the brain and nervous system have even developed! In response to the brain-heart messages, adrenaline and cortisol are produced so we have the energy to go into fight-flight survival action.

Together adrenaline and cortisol can give a woman enough strength to lift up a car that has run over a child – a superhuman energy we are capable of mobilizing when we need to go into a big stress response requiring a superhuman action.

However, the danger is that once adrenaline and cortisol are activated, there is no enzyme to switch them off. We are now at the mercy of our own adrenaline and cortisol response until it wears off – within a few minutes or within six hours.

Adrenaline and cortisol, if not used, are highly toxic.

If we don't use up our adrenaline-cortisol through movement of our large arm and leg muscles, it can be deposited in joints and muscles, causing acidity and health problems.

- Cortisol is deposited in the **joints**, which over time become stiff and arthritic

- Cortisol is deposited in the **muscles**, causing them to become hard and painful

- Adrenaline is deposited in the muscles – and under a microscope, adrenaline looks like **sharp razors**, which makes muscles tight, hard and painful

- Adrenals over-taxed through constant stress cause **exhaustion** – or constant fatigue

- Adrenaline alters the **acid secretions in the digestive tract** so we can't digest and assimilate our food properly: digestive troubles, acid reflux, irritable bowel syndrome may result

- High cortisol levels can break down the **immune system** and we get flu and colds, or worse

- High cortisol levels cause the destruction of neurons in the hippocampus: now **new memories are not created** and instead of curiosity and acquiring new knowledge, all we want is the same old routine

Is it a wonder that 90% of all illnesses are said to be related directly to stress?

So why do we have this survival response if it is so dangerous for our health?

STORY OF THE THREE CHEETAH CUBS ESCAPING A PURSUING LION

A documentary on Discovery Channel showed three cheetah cubs narrowly escaping a pursuing lion by climbing high into a tree.

The cubs were responding to a serious stress. Their sympathetic nervous system took over and they went into flight. Their adrenaline-cortisol response saved their lives.

However, it's what they did after the lion had gone that's interesting for us, because it gives us one clue about how we can de-stress after going into a stress response.

The three cubs shimmied down the tree and began to play. Each cub took turns playing the lion, while the other two practiced different escape maneuvers.

They used up their excess adrenaline-cortisol energy in action – movement of their legs, joints and body muscles.

They were also practicing successful options, which hardwired neuronal circuits in their brain and heart for handling future threats successfully.

And then when the mother cheetah returned, the three cubs exuberantly shared their success – and received maternal pleasure reinforcement for their memory bank.

Animals know how to handle stress, which is probably why we rarely or never see a traumatized cheetah!

If doing the Repatterning, return to {D} p.124

⁓

Clearly there's something we need to learn here that's important

- The cubs didn't focus on their fear and panic about facing a deadly lion

- They weren't traumatized by their life-threatening experience

- They used a life-threatening situation as a way to learn successful strategies for handling future stressful situations and they practiced creative strategies with fun

- They released the excess adrenaline and cortisol, which otherwise cause a myriad of health problems

- They shared their success with their mother and received positive re-enforcement from her – rather than her fear about what might have happened

Five steps for repatterning our stress reactions

For us – who have well-established neural pathways for negative feelings and beliefs in relation to our past experiences – the steps towards transformation are slightly different:

1. Identify the present situation as quickly as possible where we are having a stress trigger reaction.

2. Identify the past fight-flight pathway in our memory bank {C} that we still resonate with, which is re-enforcing or even causing the present stress reaction.

3. Identify the relaxing bonding parasympathetic nervous system response needed {F}.

4. Accessing our heart and prefrontal cortex, identify an intention for creating new coherent neural pathways for what is positive in the present situation {G a–f}.

5. Do one or more of the twelve actions that support the hardwiring of new positive circuits.

Twelve actions to support staying connected to the heart by overcoming automatic stress reaction *see p.130 for details*

1. Accept, free of all resistance.

2. Slow breathing.

3. Calming Cross-Overs to release deep layers of tension *See* SPIRAL UP! *book*

4. Drink pure water.

5. Magnesium chloride to relax muscles, de-stress the heart and help de-toxify the system. (Massage Magnesium chloride oil into the body: *see* drcarolyndean.com and ancientminerals.com or take an epsom salt bath).

6. Cranial Contacts to entrain brain and heart rhythms SPIRAL UP! *p.115*

7. Consciously create positive thoughts in relation to the stress situation and put them into action

8. Use dance, Yoga, Tai Chi, Chi Kung, aerobic exercise, lifting weights as a way to de-toxify excess mobilized fight-flight adrenaline and cortisol

9. Wear the ColorYourWorld Lenses (blue is calming, green is healing)

10. Hugs and loving touch

11. Meditation for slowing brainwaves, breath and the heart beat

12. Natural Remedies

4. STRESS OF THE HEART REPATTERNING

A. **Identify the present situation where you have a stress trigger reaction**

Do (a–d) in sequence.

a. **Identify the present stress situation**

Ask, "What situation do you find yourself in where you over-react or get reactive, critical or even abusive in your words or actions?"

*[**cr**] *(will be on/umb on because client resonates with this stress response).*

b. **Identify the negative feeling**

Ask, "What negative feeling do you have in response to this stressful situation?" *[**cr**] with "I feel (*name the feeling*)" *(will be on/umb on because client resonates with this stress feeling response).*

Understanding the negative feeling

The limbic midbrain is directly involved with every aspect of the fight-flight survival stress response, and especially with the feeling aspect of your thoughts. Negative thoughts you resonate with constantly activate your limbic brain survival response, which creates negative feelings like anger and fear that prepare you to run away from or fight a danger.

c. **Identify the felt sense stress response**

Ask client: "Close your eyes and think about the present stress situation. Observe your felt sense: how are you breathing in response to this situation? Where are you tensing up in response to this situation? When ready you can open your eyes." *Ask*, "What responses did you notice?" *[**cr**] with client's responses *(will be on/umb on because client resonates with these stressed body responses).*

d. **Identify the unmet need**

Say, "Your present stress response is telling you there is something you need that is not being met." *Ask*, "What need is not being met for you in this stressful situation?"

*[cr] with "I am/have *(name the need) (will be off/umb off because you don't yet resonate with having your need met).*

Understanding the present reactive stress response in relation to the past
Although this stress response appears to be in the present, in fact it relates to a past stress that is hardwired in your brain's neural circuits.

Every time something occurs in the present that is even slightly similar to that earlier stress, it reminds you of the original stress. Your system then goes into an immediate stress survival response – producing adrenaline and cortisol to help you fight or run away from what feels like a life-threatening situation – even though the original experience may have occurred twenty, thirty or forty years ago.

B. Identify the earlier experience related to the present stress
Do (a–f) in sequence.
a. Identify the earlier experience
Ask, "Do you remember an earlier experience that reminds you in some way of this present stress situation?" *[cr] *(will be on/umb on because client resonates with this past stress response).*

Understanding the significance of the earlier experience
Your stress response neural circuits are already hardwired. For instance, if a pregnant woman is under a lot of stress, by the third trimester the baby's adrenals can be enlarged!

When neural circuits are repetitively used, they fire automatically. This is helpful for survival because it provides an instant trigger response that you don't even have to think about. The problem is that these present stress responses are easily reactivated by whatever stress appears to be slightly similar to the past response. This stress firing is not in your control and, when habitually repeated, has a negative impact on your health and relationships.

b. **Identify the past unmet need associated with the earlier experience**
Explain: Every problem has an underlying need that relates to our
infancy and childhood – a genuine life-supporting need that was not
met. Some of these needs may go back hundreds of generations. Past
unmet needs we do not resonate with will not be met in the present,
which is why we continue to go into a reactive stress response.

Once we resonate with knowing our needs, expressing them and meeting
our needs, we will find that we no longer respond with a stress response
to challenging situations and people – unless required for our survival.

Ultimately knowing and meeting our needs enables us to handle life as
an adventure, providing us with new learning and growth.

(**mcs**) {1–5} for the need from the list of categories below:
1. **The need for security and survival**
   (**mcs**) {1–9}. *[**cr**] *(will be off/umb off)*.
   1. (I am cared for • I am looked after • My Life Needs are met).
   2. I feel secure.
   3. Everything is provided for.
   4. (I survive • I am successful).
   5. I am protected.
   6. I have a home.
   7. I am clothed, fed and kept warm.
   8. (I am welcomed • I belong).
   9. *Other: Ask,* "What do you need in order to feel secure about your
      survival?"

2. **Physical needs for health and energy**
   (**mcs**) {1–10}. *[**cr**] *(will be off/umb off)*.
   1. I take in and appreciate living food (mother's milk • fresh
      organically grown fruits, vegetables, nuts and seeds • pure water).
   2. I breathe pure air.
   3. (I am warm • I receive the warmth of the sun).

4. (I move for life • I am energized by movement).
5. I sleep well and wake up refreshed.
6. I receive all the (sunlight • full-spectrum light) I need.
7. I do those actions that lead to health and energy.
8. I think positive thoughts and feel good about myself and others.
9. I relax and rejuvenate myself.
10. *Other: Ask,* "What do you need for your health and energy?"

3. **The need to achieve your best, go beyond your limits and manifest your potential**
   (**mcs**) {1–12}. *[**cr**] *(will be off/umb off).*
   1. (I achieve my best • I value those who help me achieve my best).
   2. (I manifest my potential • I am successful • I enjoy going beyond my limits of what I thought was possible).
   3. I have the strength and faith to persevere through obstacles and apparent failures.
   4. I serve (others • humanity).
   5. I play (joyfully • spontaneously).
   6. I am curious.
   7. (I create beauty • I am creative in everything I do).
   8. I am confident.
   9. I am courageous.
   10. I maintain an optimistic attitude no matter what difficulties I'm facing.
   11. I put my concern for human well-being and right action before my need for (material success • the achievement of my ambitions).
   12. *Other: Ask,* "What do you need that would allow you to manifest your potential, go beyond your limits of what you think is possible, and achieve your best?"

4. **The need for love and respect in relationship**
   (**mcs**) {1–19}. *[**cr**] *(will be off/umb off).*
   1. I (receive love • give love • feel worthy of being loved) in my relationships.
   2. I have (close • affectionate • caring) relationships.

3. I belong and feel (welcomed • included • wanted).
4. I am enough.
5. I make loving connections through warm and relaxed eye contact.
6. I give and receive loving touch.
7. I am protected from harm.
8. (I have clear safe boundaries • I feel safe).
9. I am (appreciated • acknowledged • valued • respected • accepted).
10. I enjoy harmonious relationships.
11. (I have positive communication in my relationship(s) • I am heard • I hear).
12. (I am seen • I see).
13. I freely express my (truth • feelings • thoughts • ideas • humor).
14. I (relax and laugh • enjoy humor).
15. I am free to explore and return for loving touch and bonding whenever I need to.
16. My heart is open to (compassion • understanding • love).
17. (I forgive • I am forgiven • I resolve problems and grow in my capacity to love).
18. I let go of (reactiveness • blame • complaints • feeling a victim • gossip).
19. *Other: Ask,* "What do you need that would bring you love and respect in your relationship(s)?"

5. **The need for meaning, purpose, love, and happiness from within** (**mcs**) {1–20}. *[**cr**] *(will be off/umb off)*.
    1. (I feel joyful • I let go of all negative thoughts and tune in to love).
    2. I am filled with gratitude every day.
    3. (I see beauty • I see the Divine) in every aspect of the creation.
    4. I am content.
    5. (I have faith • I trust that every experience is for my highest good).
    6. I am (focused • disciplined).

7. (I pay attention to my thoughts and the stillness of my mind • I am still).
8. I accept the divine will free of resistance and fear.
9. I live my (truth • values) in action.
10. I love unconditionally.
11. (I stand for what is right • I live with integrity).
12. (I practice the presence of God • I feel spiritually connected at all times to the Divine within).
13. I let go of (self-importance • negative thoughts and feelings).
14. (I am at peace • My mind is peaceful).
15. I am receptive to Divine grace.
16. (I serve selflessly • I give generously • I find every opportunity to help others).
17. I stay conscious of the light within and the light within each person I meet.
18. I am receptive to the higher purpose and meaning of every circumstance life brings.
19. I let go of my need to get (upset • angry) about anything in this world.
20. *Other: Ask,* "What do you need for your spiritual well-being?"

c. **Identify the negative feeling associated with the earlier experience**
Ask, "What negative feeling do you imagine you had in response to (*name the earlier experience*) and your need not being met?" *[**cr**] with "I continue to feel (*name the feeling*) in the present" *(will be on/umb on)*.

Observe the relationship between this feeling response associated with the earlier experience and the feeling response in the present stress situation {A b}.

d. **Identify the negative belief associated with the earlier experience**
Ask, "What negative belief about yourself do you imagine you had as a result of (*name earlier experience*)?"
*[**cr**] *(will be on/umb on because at the moment you resonate with this belief being true).*

Understanding the belief

A belief is simply a thought you take to be true, whether it is true or not. Many things we are convinced are true are simply our own thoughts and perceptions that we have decided are true!

If you resonate with a negative belief about yourself, it is mirrored in your life and relationships, which causes a stress response that doesn't support your health and well-being.

e. **Identify the non-coherent interpretation or meaning of client's belief**
Ask, "Your belief that (*name the belief*) says something about you and/ or the person involved. We unconsciously interpret our beliefs. What meaning do you give to your belief?" *[cr] (*will be on/umb on because client resonates with this stress*).

Understanding the interpretation

One of the tasks of your higher brain pre-frontal cortex (behind your forehead) is to interpret. We give a meaning or interpretation to everything that happens to us, even to our beliefs in response to what happens to us.

For example, if I don't see the open cupboard door and hit my head on it, my **belief** may be, "I don't see what is before my eyes."

The **interpretation** of this belief may be, "You are a fool."

The interpretation I give may cause me to dislike myself and feel de-energized or to get angry and slam the cupboard door shut, or may cause me to be upset with my partner or child for leaving the door open.

We have non-coherent interpretations or coherent interpretations according to the beliefs we resonate with. The price we pay for non-coherent beliefs and interpretations is a stress response.

f. Positive belief

Explain: It is as easy to resonate with positive beliefs in relation to our earlier experiences as it is to resonate with negative beliefs and interpretations. Positive beliefs we resonate with result in positive interpretations, which cause our limbic midbrain to support our health and the achievement of our goals and intentions.

- *Ask,* "What is a positive belief you can have in relation to (*name the earlier experience*)?" *[**cr**] (*will be off/umb off*).

- *Ask,* "What is a positive interpretation of this belief?" *[**cr**] (*will be off/umb off*).

C. Identify the past fight-flight pathway client still resonates with

a. Identify the alert, fight / flight / immobilized survival response habitually re-activated in the present because the mobilized energy of the original fight-flight earlier experience was not discharged in a successful fight or flight outcome.

Explain: These survival responses may be generational patterns rather than a response client is conscious of.
(**mcs**) {1–4} for the one involved.

1. **The non-coherent alert response being re-activated in the present situation that client still resonates with**
(**mcs**) {1–7}. *[**cr**] (*will be on/umb on because client resonates with this alert stress response*).
   1. I (freeze • am incapable of action).
   2. I am anxious.
   3. I (hide • isolate myself).
   4. I am startled by (small things • anything).
   5. I can't relax because I can't (see who or what is dangerous • locate the source of a danger).
   6. I am on the alert for danger all the time.
   7. I am tense all the time.

2. **The non-coherent fight response client still resonates with**
   (**mcs**) {1–12}. *[**cr**] *(will be on/umb on because client resonates with this fight stress response).*
   1. (I am defensive • I overreact).
   2. I am overly assertive.
   3. (I am quarrelsome • I pick quarrels).
   4. I am (impatient • angry • frustrated • enraged).
   5. I easily become violent.
   6. I am hyper-nervous.
   7. I am a caretaker for everyone.
   8. I am (over-controlling • dominating).
   9. (I am excessively talkative • I interrupt (*name person*) before he/she has finished talking).
   10. (I make others wrong • I tell (*name person*) that he/she is wrong • I blame and criticize).
   11. I use sex to discharge my anger.
   12. I can't keep still.

3. **The non-coherent flight list response client still resonates with**
   (**mcs**) {1–9}. *[**cr**] *(will be on/umb on because client resonates with this flight stress response).*
   1. (I am unable to avoid dangerous situations • I habitually put myself in dangerous situations).
   2. I run away from situations in a panic, unable to think clearly.
   3. (I get in a panic • I am chronically anxious).
   4. I turn to (food • alcohol • drugs • cigarettes • sex • sleep • gambling other) as a way to escape.
   5. (I become ill as a way to avoid a threatening situation • I run away from life).
   6. I stop (hearing • seeing • tasting • smelling • feeling) as a way to avoid a threatening situation.
   7. I escape by being depressed.

8. (I can't get going • I can't move into action • I can't run away • I can't avoid danger.)
9. I cry as a way of handling any emotionally charged situation I can't cope with.

4. **The non-coherent immobilized response client still resonates with** (**mcs**) {1–7}. *[cr] *(will be on/umb on because client resonates with this immobilized response).*
    1. I (collapse • feel dead • go into shock).
    2. I (numb out • disassociate • disembody).
    3. I am in an altered state of consciousness in which I do whatever others want me to do.
    4. I am depressed.
    5. (I feel fragmented • I survive by fragmenting myself into different personality responses).
    6. (I feel drugged • I am passive • I am unable to go into action).
    7. I am (rigid • paralyzed).

D. **Read or tell the story of the three cheetah cubs** *p.112*
   Ask, "What does this story mean for you?" *[cr] with "I *(name the positive meaning)" (will be off/umb off).*

E. **Identify the coherent survival responses of your sympathetic nervous system (SNS)**
   (**mcs**) {1–4} for the one needed.
   1. **The coherent alert response**
      (**mcs**) {1–12}. *[cr] *(will be off/umb off because client doesn't yet resonate with the coherent alert response).*
      1. I am alert and ready for action.
      2. I am alert yet relaxed.
      3. I orient myself away from danger.
      4. I orient myself towards what is nourishing, bonding and supports my survival.
      5. I am curious.
      6. If no threat is present I immediately relax.

7. I quickly locate where there is danger and who is involved.
8. I am confident.
9. I am able to identify and meet any challenge.
10. I access a wide range of options and reactions.
11. If there is no threat I release residual activated energy by moving, trembling or shaking out.
12. I easily move through states of tense hyper-vigilance and relaxed alertness.

2. **The coherent fight response**
(**mcs**) {1–6}. *[**cr**] *(will be off/umb off because client doesn't resonate with the coherent fight response).*
   1. I set clear boundaries with (power • strength • confidence • love).
   2. I stand on my own two feet.
   3. I am ready to face any challenge with (clarity • focused attention • appropriate decision-making • excitement • the ability to see all sides of the situation).
   4. After meeting a challenge I dissipate any residual mobilized energy by (shaking • trembling • moving • walking • running • exercising • dancing).
   5. I share my success in handling a challenge with (*name person*) and relax into love-bonding once more.
   6. I defend myself.

3. **The coherent flight response**
(**mcs**) {1–4}. *[**cr**] *(will be off/umb off because you doesn't yet resonate with the coherent flight response).*
   1. I move away from dangerous situations.
   2. I am clear and oriented when facing a danger so I know the best way to handle the difficulty.
   3. After successfully avoiding a threat I (shake • tremble • move) in order to dissipate any residual mobilized energy.
   4. After successfully avoiding a threat I discharge excess mobilized energy by playing out different ways of successfully escaping and sharing my success with (others).

4. **The coherent immobilization response**
   (**mcs**) {1–2}. *[**cr**] *(will be off/umb off because client doesn't resonate with the coherent immobilization response).*
   1. When facing possible (death • overwhelm), I accept that my body knows how to become temporarily immobilized for my protection.
   2. When I become immobilized in response to a life-threatening situation, I know that I can recover and (shake • tremble • move) so I feel relaxed and embodied once more and capable of immediate action to save myself.

F. **Identify the coherent parasympathetic nervous system (PNS) response needed**
   (**mcs**) {1–15}. *[**cr**] *(will be off/umb off because client doesn't resonate with relaxing out of stress at this time).*
   1. I am nurtured and my emotional needs are taken care of.
   2. I receive loving touch, which relaxes me.
   3. I feel relaxed when I touch others.
   4. After dealing with a threat I totally relax and enjoy life again.
   5. I trust that all good things are coming to me.
   6. (I relax • I am calm • I experience life as being safe).
   7. I freely move all body parts.
   8. My survival needs are taken care of.
   9. I sleep peacefully.
   10. I am ready to handle any change or challenge life presents me with in a calm and relaxed way.
   11. I have a positive attitude towards others.
   12. I feel safe in the here and now.
   13. (I am relaxed yet alert • I resolve my constrictions).
   14. I shake out any residual tension.
   15. I (am secure • trust).

G. **Identify the heart and higher mind response (versus the SNS stress response)**
   Do (a–f) in sequence.

a. **The pause**
   *[cr] with "In this/any stressful situation, I take a pause and relax into 'And this too shall pass'" *(will be off/umb off)*.

b. **Accept the reality of what is**
   *[cr] with "I accept the reality of what is. This situation is what it is and getting stressed about it wont change it" *(will be off/umb off)*.

c. **The response**
   *[cr] with "I choose how I respond, whether I react negatively or come from my heart, whether I resist or stay calm" *(will be off/umb off)*.

d. **Options for action**
   Ask, "What are all the possible options for action open to you?" Client names all possible options. *[cr] with "I am clear about all the possible options for action – whether positive or negative" *(will be off/umb off)*.

e. **Positive action**
   *[cr] with "(I go into right action based on listening to my heart's inner knowing • I am responsible for my own right action, no matter how *(name person)* chooses to act or react • I speak my truth and name my needs kindly, lovingly and free of fear/anger • I set clear boundaries from my heart on negative behavior)" *(will be off/umb off)*.

f. **The positive feeling**
   Ask, "How would this new way of responding make you feel?"
   *[cr] with "I feel *(name the positive feeling)*" *(will be off/umb off because at the moment you do not resonate with a positive, non-stress way of feeling)*.

H. Identify the Energizing Option needed
Acupuncture points without needles

The following Energizing Option – eight acupuncture points to balance your meridians without needles – aims to support you as you meet your challenges on the way to achieving your vision.

The points:

If you have studied Resonance Repatterning, you can muscle check which of the points is needed, the sequence for doing them in, whether the left and/or right side is needed, and for details on whether the ColorYourWorld Torch and/or Tuning Fork is to be used on the point(s). You can also check if the CYW Lenses are needed.

For non-Resonance Repatterning people, read what each point does and choose the point you intuitively feel will most help in the present situation. If you do not have the CYW Torch or Tuning Forks, use a finger contact on the point and hold it for longer, hopefully feeling the energy. *See ResonanceRepatterning.net > Store for CYW Torch, CYW Lenses and Tuning Forks and > Home Study Course for Inner Cultivation*

- **Earth Element, Stomach Meridian:** This point is about two inches below the knee crease on the outer edge of the leg. Slide your finger into the muscles towards your shin bone and see if you can feel the point.

  This point is called Leg Three Miles. The ancient Chinese Acupuncturists believed that this point supports longevity and revitalizes your energy. It is wonderful to use this point when you need endurance, stamina, stability and especially when you are worried about harvesting positive results from what you have done, or feel there will be no harvest for the work you have put in. This point will help strengthen your resolve to keep moving forward, keeping you grounded and energized for your onward journey.

- **Metal Element, Lung Meridian:** The point is under the clavicle where it meets the shoulder.

  This point is called Cloud Gate. It is uplifting, helping you reconnect to the Divine within yourself, to see through the clouds of difficulties, to have faith that the sun is still shining beyond the clouds.

- **Water Element, Bladder Meridian:** The point is on either side of your spine at the top of your neck, just under the ridge of your skull bone, on the large trapezius neck muscle. Your two fingers will be about an inch away from the spine, one on each side.

   This point is called Heavenly Pillar. It gives you the strength, power, calmness and energy to handle the resistance of your challenges and gives you the inner strength to keep reaching for your vision.

- **Wood Element, Liver Meridian:** The point is underneath the middle of the ribs on both sides.

   This point is called Gate of Hope. It gives you the hope, optimism and vision to handle your stress with positive action, coherent plans and decisions that are aligned with your vision.

- **Fire Element, Heart Protector Meridian:** With the palm facing up, the point is found on the middle of the wrist in the hollow that you can feel when you flex your hand towards you.

   This point is called Great Mound. The burial ground for emperors – a place of great power. Great Mound gives you a renewed sense of confidence, safety, trust and love when you are feeling vulnerable or when you need to call on the strength of your generational history for support and vision.

- **Fire Element, Triple Heater Meridian:** With your arm bent and the palm facing the shoulder, this point is about an inch above the tip of the elbow on the back of the upper arm.

   This point is called Heaven Well. It strengthens the mind and spirit by helping you recharge yourself through connection to the divine – an inexhaustible well that has only good to bring.

- **Fire Element, Heart Meridian**: This point is at your armpits, behind the tendon – children like to place their thumbs on these points!

  This point is called Utmost Source. It is a wonderful point to use when there is chaos, confusion, agitation or when you no longer feel oriented towards your vision. Do this point when you need to reconnect deeply to the ultimate source of love, compassion and consciousness within yourself.

- **Fire Element, Small Intestine Meridian:** Slide your finger down the outer edge of the little finger and feel the notch before the base joint of the little finger.

  This point is called Forward Valley. It gives you the drive and perseverance to transform life's problems into challenging adventures. It empowers you to sort out what is rich and to act on what enriches your life. It helps you move forward fearlessly and with will-power when you have much to sort out, helping you conserve your energy by doing what is important, and leaving the rest.

How To:
- (**mcs**) for the sequence for doing the point.s
- (**mcs**) whether the point(s) need to be done on the left and/or right side.
- (**mcs**) whether the CYW Torch or Tuning Forks are needed on the points. (**mcs**) for details.
- (**mcs**) if the CYW Lenses are needed and for details on the color(s).

I. **Identify which of the following twelve actions is needed for anchoring new positive circuits in the neo-cortex, the limbic midbrain and the cerebellum of the reptilian brain to support a coherent heart response**
All of these actions are important. In any stressful situation do as many of them as you remember. Some of them can be done in almost any situation –

in the car, at work or at home. Others can be done after you are free from the challenging situation.(**mcs**) for details.

Some of these twelve actions may be used as the Energizing Option for the session. Doing them and understanding why they are important will help reinforce them in your mind so you automatically remember to use them in the stress situation itself.

1. **Acceptance free of all resistance**
    Say, "I accept (*name the present situation*), free of resistance."

    In stressful situations the trigger response usually takes you into upset, blame, criticism, panic, etc. This causes yet more stress and another adrenaline response on top of the one you already have.

    Acceptance activates the parasympathetic nervous system (PNS), which supports immediate and often seemingly miraculous healing and repair – freedom from pain, self-healing, or the strength to face great suffering with a sense of inner calm. It is said that with acceptance free of resistance, 'the sword thrust is reduced to a pinprick'.

    Acceptance does not mean we are passive. Acceptance always involves right action. People who survive extreme situations (for example, airplane crashes in remote mountain areas) are those who accept the reality of what is and then go into action.

    There is a story about a man who was cutting down branches with his chainsaw. Suddenly the saw slipped and cut through his thigh, almost to the bone. His sons were about to take him to the hospital, but the father told them to hold the skin and muscles together and to let him be still. He then started saying, "I accept free of resistance..." and he named everything he had done: his lack of balance; holding the chainsaw in an awkward way; the slipping of the chainsaw; the pain as it went through his thigh. He kept repeating "I accept free of resistance..." repeating each action and feeling. After about two hours of this acceptance repetition, there was nothing but a hairpin scar.

A Resonance Repatterning practitioner remembered this story when a group of thirteen dogs attacked her. She had bites that went right to the bone. The doctors were amazed and mystified that her healing was extraordinary – within a few weeks the scars were hardly visible.

2. **Breathing**
Slowing down the breath to about five breaths per minute activates the parasympathetic nervous system, which calms the adrenal stress response and allows for healing and regeneration. Do nose breathing and the Control Pause Breath to help slow down your breathing. *See* SPIRAL UP! *p.172*

3. **Calming Cross-Overs** *See* SPIRAL UP! *p.115*

4. **Drink pure water**
Water flushes out toxins and acidity. During stressful situations we need to drink more water, which is also needed for conducting electrical impulses throughout the body. It is excellent to put a pinch of Himalayan crystal salt into each 8 oz glass of water. *See ResonanceRepatterning.net/ chloes-thoughts-salt-that-heals-salt-that-kills for article on crystal salt and solay*

5. **Magnesium chloride oil massage and foot bath** *See p.157*
Stress depletes magnesium. Massaging magnesium chloride oil into the skin relaxes muscle tension, de-stresses the heart (a muscle) and helps to detoxify the system. *See Ameriden.com for high-quality magnesium chloride oil and drcarolyndean.com (or Amazon) for an ionic magnesium chloride that is 100% absorbed at the cellular level and does not have a laxative effect.*

6. **Cranial Contact**
Place your fourth, middle and index fingers lightly on your forehead, about half way between your hairline and your eyebrows. This has a deeply calming effect as it recalibrates your cranial rhythms, which become disordered in stress-response situations.

7. **Positive thought**
   In a full-blown stress response our thoughts are negative and we become reactive, saying or doing things we regret. It is our thoughts that set off our sympathetic nervous system adrenaline response, and the stress is then further compounded with yet more negative thoughts, feelings and actions.

   When in a stressful situation, think, say or do something positive and observe what happens: positive-feeling brain chemicals are released and a calming, relaxing, bonding, self-healing response is activated by our parasympathetic nervous system.

   Dan Millman, the author of *Way of the Peaceful Warrior,* related how he was once crossing the Golden Gate Bridge while being tailgated by an impatient and angry man. There was nothing Dan could do to get out of his way. When Dan reached the tollbooth, he paid both for himself and the tailgating car behind him. When the lady told the man that his toll had been paid for, the man's attitude instantly shifted: he started waving and smiling. Clearly he was blown away by Dan Millman's positive action in response to his irritation and tailgating!

   Ask, "What positive thoughts, words or actions can you think of in your present stress situation?"

8. **Dance and/or calming Yoga**
   Moving the large muscles of your arms and legs uses up the excess mobilized adrenaline and cortisol hyperactive energy. These movements lead to endorphins of joy that boost your immune system as well as preventing adrenaline and cortisol from being deposited in your muscles and joints. Put on some music and move, vigorously. Slow Yoga stretches are also great.

9. **ColorYourWorld Lenses**
   ColorYourWorld Lenses use roscolene gels with the same frequencies developed by Dr. Dinshah in the 1930s for self-healing. The green and blue lenses have a calming effect on the mind.

This powerful Energizing Option transmits frequencies of color directly to the hypothalamus of the brain. The lenses may be worn for a few minutes or more, but sometimes even a few seconds are enough. *See ResonanceRepatterning.net e-Store*

10. **Loving touch**
Hugs and loving touch activate the parasympathetic nervous system, which calms the stress response and supports digestion, regeneration and bonding.

Gently massage your legs, arms, face and neck.

11. **Meditation**
Sit with a straight spine, very still. When you breathe gently through your nose, using your solar plexus, and taking about five breaths per minute, your brainwaves begin to slow down. Gradually let your mind become still. Feel the tranquility.

12. **Natural Remedies**
If you are knowledgable on natural remedies or a book that may help, share this with your client.

J. **RR Practitioners now recheck *[cr] statements and confirm any change in resonance**

HOW TO USE THE FIVE STEPS AND TWELVE ACTIONS IN YOUR DAILY LIFE
EVEN IF YOU HAVE NOT YET ATTENDED A RESONANCE REPATTERNING SEMINAR

When any stress hits you:

- Immediately do {G a–f} + an Energizing Option to change your resonance.

- Do any of the Twelve Actions that you can remember! Acceptance free of resistance and breathing are always the best place to begin!

- Do one or more of the letters along with an Energizing Option for shifting the resonance. For example:
  A + B + H
  A + C + H
  A + D + H
  E + F + H
  E + I + H
  F + I + H

RR SESSIONS: If you would like to receive the complete Repatterning with a professional Resonance Repatterning Practitioner, in person or over the phone, go to ResonanceRepatterning.net > Sessions for RR Institute Practitioners worldwide who have listed themselves on the RRI website.

RR SEMINARS: If you would like to attend Resonance Repatterning seminars in person or online, so you can use RR effectively on yourself and/or others, go to ResonanceRepatterning.net > Seminars for the list of teachers endorsed by the Resonance Repatterning Institute to teach.

5. DEPRESSION OF THE HEART –
AND HOPE

In the landscape of spring, nothing is better or worse. The
flowering branches grow naturally, long or short.

Ancient Chinese poem

If we have the means within ourselves to be happy under the most challenging of
circumstances, why are millions of people unhappy and suffering the pain of what
I call depression of the heart?

Many of us, who don't think of ourselves as depressed, do in fact have non-
coherent habits that may be the way we unconsciously choose to keep
depression – or boredom and the feeling that life is meaningless – at bay.

What is depression
When the mind is scattered, speeded up, not focused, depression is the result.
Depression is a way of thinking and feeling: I feel down, negative, hopeless,
bored, worthless, unloved, unhappy, despondent, overwhelmed by life, devalued,
exhausted, suicidal, and life is meaningless.

These non-coherent dejected thoughts are frequencies that activate
corresponding brain-body biochemicals, which are also frequencies.

Brain-body biochemicals create feelings and body responses that match each of
our thoughts, whether positive or negative.

Healing depression of the heart

From the spiritual perspective, there is only the positive in life: relaxation, hope, happiness, inspiration, faith, pleasure, peace of mind, tolerance, courage, optimism, loving communication, etc.

Darkness is the absence of light. If we don't resonate with the positive – with the light – we automatically experience its shadow – the dark and what is negative: tension, stress, unhappiness, boredom, pain, a scattered mind, disharmony, anger, fear, pessimism, conflict, quarrels **and** depression.

Our present is based on our past: mostly positive if we experienced the positive and mostly negative if we experienced the negative. True healing of the pain of depression involves transforming our resonance with non-coherent, negative thought frequencies – the unconscious perceptions, beliefs and feelings in response to painful experiences in the womb, our infancy and early childhood. And coming back into natural resonance with the positive so we are able to focus on and perceive what is positive in every aspect of our life and relationships.

THE SENOI AND YEQUANA PEOPLE

In *The Biology of Transcendence*, Joseph Chilton Pearce talks about a small group of aboriginal people called the Senoi, who used to live in the jungles of Malaya.

Chilton Pearce writes that "the Senoi lived with unquestioned acceptance of each other, without judgment or censure, in a natural and spontaneous manner that was simply the only response they knew."

He relates that "the Senoi refrained from judging self or others not from some noble virtue but because their minds, not having been formed in the same manner as ours, simply didn't function that way – never having been judged or restrained, they had no concept of either and no neural paths for relating in these ways."

To the Senoi, how a child or adult acted was accepted in the same way that you accept the direction of the wind or the slant of sunlight. It was just what it was!

A similar group to the Senoi are the Yequana of Venezuela. The anthropologist Jean Liedloff lived with them and wrote about them. She explained that no child deliberately injured another or was unpleasant toward anyone because they had never seen an adult injure someone or be unpleasant. She writes, "Deciding what another person should do, regardless of his age, is outside the Yequana vocabulary of behaviors. There is great interest in what everyone does, but no impulse to influence – let alone coerce – anyone."

If doing the Repatterning, return to {B a} p.168

These two groups represent something extraordinary:
- Unquestioned acceptance

- No judgment or censure

- Never seeing anyone being unpleasant toward another person

- Never getting someone to do what you think they should do – no coercion!

How many of us have ever experienced this kind of modeling?

Let's look at depression of the heart from three points of view:
1. The primary mother-infant bond
2. The Five Elements of Chinese Acupuncture
3. Our biochemistry

1. The primary mother-infant bond
We know that we model ourselves after our primary caregiver, usually the mother – starting in the womb, and continuing in infancy and childhood –

and also with the father and siblings, followed by teachers, peer groups, friends, people we admire, the media – for better or for worse.

As a result of the modeling most of us have received, we **tell** our children and others **what to do** rather than **model** for them **how to be** – as do the Senoi and Yequana people.

A mother's intuitive knowing
Every now and then we do hear of someone who manifests the power of positive modeling, like the mother who intuitively decided to carry her infant into the bathroom with her each time she had to use the toilet. Within a few days, her newborn spontaneously urinated and defecated in sync with her!

It's all frequencies: children learn by bringing their frequencies into sync with their parents' frequencies – positive or negative. And when the mother is in sync with her child, she intuitively knows her child's needs.

For example, an anthropologist was mystified and asked how African tribal women knew exactly when their infant was ready to 'go to the bathroom,' at which point they squatted their child down in the bush. The African women were equally mystified and asked the anthropologist: "Why wouldn't we know? Don't *you* know when *you* want to go?"

When frequencies are in sync there is no separation. This is why a mother and child need as much physical contact as possible. In Africa the infant is always in contact with the caregivers for the first year of his or her life, carried around day and night by the mother or a sibling. Mother and child are bonded as one and the mother therefore instinctively knows her infant's needs.

But more than this, in-sync frequencies with the caregiver allows the infant to download huge amounts of knowledge in the first few years of life – more perhaps than we download throughout the rest of our life. The infant learns about life – the environment, relationships – through contact with the mother, experiencing her movements, rhythm, connection with others, work. She is the infant's model of how to live.

As we see with the Senoi and Yequana, the ideal modeling the infant needs is based on love, acceptance and non-judgment.

When modeling is not based on acceptance and love, our energy constricts and we become out of sync or depressed. When this happens, we can no longer bond with another's field of energy in a way that amplifies connection to what is positive and life-giving.

As a consequence we experience separation instead of unending oneness. And this is where the depression of the heart begins.

Shame

We've all watched infants and young children with awe: the wonder of everything, the uncontained energy, the excitement, enthusiasm, total involvement, focus and the ability to create play from whatever is available. The child is intent on discovering his or her world.

What happens to this bubbling, spontaneous, charismatic life energy? Why and how do we lose touch with it and with ourselves?

In the Western world, by the time infants are two years old, they have heard the word **No** about 20,000 times – or as another statistic puts it, the infant hears a 'No' or a 'Don't' on average once every nine minutes.

In one study a tape recorder was attached to each child. The researchers discovered that most of the communications involved telling children what they couldn't do or telling them off for doing what they had been told they shouldn't do!

But it is not just language. Researchers say the mother's facial expression is as powerful as her language. She can show her displeasure just by her look or her posture or how she turns away from her child.

The great philosopher and educator, Rudolf Steiner, says that shame disrupts the slow development of the child's growing awareness of his or her body, which should happen naturally by about the age of six. A premature awareness of their body, he says, results in a rejection of the self as a whole being – in other words it leads to the inability to accept one's self.

Sacrificing involvement and exploration of life
The infant's psyche needs the bond with the mother even at the price of pulling away from its enthusiastic involvement and exploration of life.

Growth of the higher brain (the pre-frontal cortex) depends to a great extent on mother-infant interactions in the first nine months after birth. This makes bonding a priority over new learning and exploration.

To break the bond with the mother brings isolation and inhibits cellular growth of the higher pre-frontal brain. Isolated by her non-acceptance and judgments, the infant moves into fear: fear of losing the bond of love that is its survival.

Then shame sets in: shame that I have displeased my mother; shame that love, even for a moment, is withdrawn because of something I did. 'I am worthless' is a common belief that too many of us think is true and resonate with.

Once shame is imprinted, the child goes into hesitation and self-doubt. The poet William Blake writes, "Were the sun and moon to doubt, they'd immediately go out." So with us, some of our light goes out when we taste the depression of self-doubt and shame. Restraint on our natural life-energy follows.

Author and researcher, Allen Schore, writes that this shame-stress is characterized by elevated cortisol levels – an adrenaline fight-flight stress response. The same is found in children experiencing abandonment and separation anxiety from their mother.

Synchronizing frequencies through loving face-gazing and eye-gazing
Face and eye-gazing is essential for creating neural connections between the emotional limbic brain and the pre-frontal cortex, which supports higher brain development, bonding with love and communication.

When an infant experiences separation-stress from its mother, it leads to an avoidance of mutual face-gazing. If not given, or if face-gazing is given when the mother is scolding the child, the child begins to avoid eye contact and experiences face-gazing as threatening.

Gazing into the eyes is an expression of love and creates connection to others. Gazing is how we bond, how we experience unity in love, how we express our curiosity and interest in those around us.

If eye-gazing is threatening or feels unsafe, it impacts our capacity to bond in all our future relationships.

And a further complication is added because of modern technology. Mothers and fathers are now over-focused on their iPhone, texting, talking on their phone, gazing at their computer, and the infant is now over-focused on his or her own iPad! No one is looking at each other!

We see that for most people the underlying basis for experiencing unity and love (by bringing our frequencies into sync with our primary caregivers through eye-gazing) is missing or seriously lacking.

Gazing into each other's eyes is something that brings a deep sense of joy and pleasure with every newborn. It energizes the mother, father and the child.

Eye-gazing is also something we do when we are in love. Gazing into the eyes of one we love is about oneness, uplift and joy versus separation and depression. Gazing into the eyes of one we love is about accessing the spirit that is love.

Primary conflict and depression

Chilton Pearce says that confusion and depression in the child come about when two most important needs are not met. The first need is that the bond with the caregiver is maintained at all costs and the second need is that the world is available to be explored.

When these two possibilities are lacking, it leads to confusion, and depression of the infant's life energy.

The mother, or primary caregiver, is the support and guide for the child but is also the one who says 'No' and 'Don't' and stops the child in his/her drive to explore the world freely.

The Senoi and Yequana don't live with this double bind that leads to the child's first sense of isolation and alienation from its mother, and shame that the infant is not acceptable to its mother.

Pre-frontal brain development

The pre-frontals, the part of our neo-cortex behind our brow, gives us our higher brain awareness, reasoning and ability to see all sides of an issue. The pre-frontals are associated with our humanity and spiritual evolution – and their development is largely determined by mother-infant interactions in the first eighteen months after birth.

Growth of the pre-frontals also depends on stimuli from the environment – and the infant's environment is primarily its mother – through touching her, seeing her, hearing her voice, smelling her fragrance, tasting her milk and moving with all her movements.

Our four brains and depression

We have four brains: the reptilian, limbic, neo-cortex and the highest development of all, our pre-frontals.

When our pre-frontal lobes are in control, we are involved and fully engaged in every moment of our life and we expand our consciousness, constantly open to new learning and exciting possibilities.

But for most of us, our lower reptilian survival brain and our emotionally reactive limbic brain are in control. These two lower brains are for instantaneous survival where no higher thinking is involved, and are meant to be in the service of our higher brain reasoning: our neo-cortex and pre-frontals.

Summary of bonding issues and depression
Perhaps we now have some idea why depression of the heart is the major problem of our age:

- Mothers no longer spend the first few years of their newborn's life with them – often returning to work within two weeks

- Too often babies are not breastfed, or are weaned prematurely before the infant is ready

- Babies are not in physical contact with the mother for the first nine months of their life and there is a lack of skin to skin contact with the mother

- Eye-gazing and face-gazing from birth are missing or seriously lacking

- Babies are separated from the mother, often as soon as they are born, or when they are put in a separate room or sent to pre-school

- The inadequate modeling the parents themselves received is generally superimposed on their infant: whether through No, Don't, neglect, punishment, verbal abuse or worse – physical and sexual abuse

- Children don't have enough loving family time together, talking, sharing, eating and playing together

- Often the positive father modeling may be inadequate when men work long hours and only see their children on weekends

The reality is we didn't receive the unconditional love, care, harmony and acceptance that we see modeled by the Senoi and Yequana.

But all is not lost.

Everything we have experienced is in our mind and heart. And the non-coherent out-of-sync frequencies of our mind and heart can become coherent – can move back into sync with what is positive and life-giving.

We can re-parent ourselves and our children.

2. ## The Five Elements of Chinese Acupuncture and depression of the heart

The consequences of any inadequate, non-coherent modeling shows up energetically as disharmony in the flow of our Five Element Acupuncture Meridian system.

The Five Elements of Chinese Acupuncture – known as Wood, Fire, Earth, Metal and Water – give us a map for understanding frequencies and how to bring our frequencies back into balance for physical, emotional and mental well-being, no matter what we received or did not receive as infants.

When the infant loses it natural bond to self and its caregivers as a result of separation, lack of eye- and face-gazing or eye-gazing that is associated with scolding and punishment, judgments, non-acceptance, neglect or even abuse, we will see disturbances in the natural harmony of the five Elements.

Depression of the heart is a sense of separation from the divine unity of all beings, and leads to a feeling of disconnection from the joy of life. It manifests in different ways according to the primary Element energy that loses its natural harmony.

The depression of the Wood Element shows up in different Wood ways:
*   Anger or rage.

*   A profound sense of hopelessness that anything good is possible.

- A loss of vision for our life.

- A deep pessimism about being acceptable or of ever being able to grow to our fullest potential and create the change we want.

- Self-judgments, judging others or feeling judged by others: nothing and no one are ever enough. There is always something wrong.

- The wood-depressed person may seek escape from the pain of their hopelessness through drugs and alcohol.

In Chapter 1 of LIVING IN TUNE WITH YOUR LIGHT, we read the story of the young man whose leg was amputated and how he became enraged, hopeless, judgmental, and turned to alcohol and drugs – all Wood Element responses.

We can see now that the young man's loss of his leg was about healing his lack of self-acceptance and the loss of what he had identified himself with. His lack of self-acceptance as with all of us begins from infancy. The pattern of non-self-acceptance is simply re-enforced by painful experiences.

His lack of self-acceptance manifested as judgments: he judged himself as less than. He judged the doctors and the parents of children who had met with accidents as incapable of understanding what their children were going through. His life felt like it was over and he had a deep Wood hopelessness and pessimism.

Our pain and problems challenge us to heal, to become whole, to love and to accept ourselves and others, to live in harmony with our world like the Senoi.

Once the young man discovered his true goal in life, serving those who had lost parts of themselves as he had, he was able to accept himself and others.

He re-discovered his light and his heart's ability to love and be loved. His anger-depression of the heart lifted. He was healed.

The beginning of healing for a Wood depressed person is through hope, standing up for what is right, having a vision for their life and going into action to manifest that vision.

The depression of the Fire Element shows up in different Fire ways:
- A Fire depression puts out the fire of our innate joy and laughter – our joy in connecting with all people with harmony and fun.

- We lose the trust that people are safe and unconditionally loving.

- We no longer receive pleasure from bonding with people by gazing at each person with interest, looking into their eyes with love and acceptance, and experiencing our innate unity and bond with all beings – as do the Senoi and Yequana.

- The Heart Meridian is about connection to the Emperor of the heart within, where we are aligned to our essence: we are conscious and aware, we naturally do the right thing at the right time effortlessly, we radiate an atmosphere of peace and compassion and create order out of chaos.

With depression of the heart, we may have control issues (over controlling or out of control). We may swing between chaos and over-control as we try to bring order back into our life. We may close our heart to relationship in order to avoid whatever hurt, pain and disappointment we have experienced.

An example of healing for a Fire depressed child
A woman asked her friend, who had just attended the Resonance Repatterning Fundamentals seminar, if she would give her eight-year-old child a session. The child had tried to commit suicide on many occasions and after one more attempt, he absolutely refused to see yet another psychiatrist. Desperate, the mother phoned her friend, and the child said he wanted the session with this family friend.

Feeling a little insecure, but using what she had just learned, she muscle checked what would help the child. But everything she checked came up with an *(off)* muscle response – meaning that it would not help the child.

Finally her muscle checking indicated that he needed just one simple Energizing Option: gobbledygook sounds. Trusting herself and her muscle checking, she and the child began speaking in gobbledygook nonsense language, until both of them were laughing and tears were pouring down their cheeks. Her muscle checking then indicated the session was complete.

The next day the mother phoned up excitedly to say her child was playing again and singing.

The Energizing Option of gobbledy gook sounds had opened a door to the child's Fire Element: play, fun, laughter, loving connection with another human being and acceptance. As a result the boy once more reconnected to the natural joy of the child: exploring his world, playing and singing.

Talking with one psychiatrist after another about his suicide attempts couldn't activate the child's Fire Element.

The beginning of healing for a Fire depressed person is through connection, trust, love and laughter, excitement, play and fun.

The depression of the Earth Element shows up in different Earth ways:
As the Earth Element corresponds directly to our relationship with our mother, it begs certain questions: Did we feel nurtured by our mother? Was our mother unconditionally accepting of us? Were we separated from our mother? Did we feel grounded and anchored to our body and our environment through our connection to our mother? Did we feel neglected and abandoned by our mother? Did we have the eye-gazing we needed with her? Did we have eye-gazing when she was angry with us or scolding us? Did we feel abused by her?

Without mothering support, we may move into an Earth depression:
• The lack of acceptance we perceived may begin the process of our rejecting our body – no longer seeing ourselves as one whole being: body, mind and soul.

- Depression of the Earth may act out as food issues – excessive eating, insufficient eating or not being nourished by what we take in.

- In the Earth Element depression, we tend to lose our center of equilibrium: we may feel that we don't belong in our family, in any group or even in the world. We may feel stuck outside ourselves, disconnected from ourselves, not in our body.

- We may tend to nurture others to the point of exhaustion, feeling that it is our responsibility to take care of everyone else's needs. This kind of nurturance of others brings no satisfaction and may lead to resentment that our needs in turn are not being met.

- We may be unable to receive nurturance from others, or constantly need nurturance and yet nothing satisfies us, nothing is ever enough.

- We may feel dependent on others or constantly needy or we may disconnect from our needs by living an isolated, stringent lifestyle.

The beginning of healing for us as an Earth-depressed person is through being centered and at peace within ourself, accepting and being nurtured by all that life gives. And by giving generously to those in need free of any desire for a reward. It may involve resonating with the abundance of life by harvesting the riches of all our life experiences – which includes the riches of challenging experiences – and opening our heart to receive this abundance.

The depression of the Metal Element shows up in different Metal ways:
- The Metal Element corresponds directly to our relationship with our father, both worldly and spiritual, who supports the expression of our authentic self – our spirit.

- When we aren't respected and valued, or when we feel demeaned and devalued, we lose our sense of self-worth. When we disconnect from our authentic self, from our own spirit, from the Divine, we no longer value who we are and what we do and we may sink into a void-like depression where life has no meaning.

- This void-like depression is in total contrast to the experience of the Senoi, who live in an unbroken relationship with the Divine. They feel this force of love through which everything in life works for the higher good.

- In the Metal Element depression, where the spiritual connection is broken, we may feel a deep sadness or grief; we may feel that we have no spiritual support. This dark night of the soul may bring a profound sense of emptiness and loss of meaning. We may feel cut off from life's higher purpose and lose our faith that there is good in all things. When we lose our inner connection, our self-worth plummets and we may sink into a void.

The beginning of healing for a Metal Element depression is through connection to the Divine and valuing ourselves and others as spiritual beings: we feel inspired by the possibility for spiritual growth and realize that ultimately everything we have experienced has a higher meaning and purpose for us.

The depression of the Water Element shows up in different Water ways:
- Exhaustion and the inability to move forward – like sitting on a powerful motor bike, revving it up to take off, but it doesn't move.

- A Water Element depression involves fear, panic and even desperation.

- There is a loss of willpower to direct and conserve our energy: we waste our energy, money and resources, get into debt or we don't channel our energy or use it for manifesting our spiritual purpose and potential

- There's a feeling of powerlessness; a lack of control over mind and feelings; everything in our life feels overwhelming. We may feel we're in an uncontained flood and we lack the courage to help ourselves.

The beginning of healing for us as a Water-depressed person is through using our willpower to contain our energy and direct it towards manifesting our potential as human beings – to manifest our spiritual purpose and what we have come to this world to achieve.

3. **Biochemistry and depression – the final step-down**

Our inadequate, non-coherent modeling and Five Element imbalance shows up physiologically as biochemical imbalances. And our biochemistry directly affects our mood, feelings and our level of depression.

When our frequencies are out of sync with what is positive and life-giving, it is reflected both in our lower brain responses and our biochemistry.

Although drugs can sometimes be life-saving, they cannot create coherence in our frequencies – in fact just the opposite. Their side effects create yet more non-coherence.

It is a matter of flexibility: many people are trying natural means first, if there is time, and receiving support from drugs when absolutely unavoidable. That said, it is important to check with your doctor if you have concerns.

Some natural remedies for depression

- The five natural remedies provided below are associated with our brain.

- The sixth remedy is specific for the heart.

- In addition, there are a minimum of Thirteen self-help ways for handling depression naturally (with the support of your primary caregiver).

These are simple well-researched remedies we can begin to integrate into our lifestyle that can benefit overall health. We can observe for ourselves whether they help with depression.

It is important that each one of us is aware of our biochemistry and natural ways to keep it balanced.

Equally important: be aware when you need extra support from professionals and always play it safe and get their opinion if in any doubt.

Five biochemicals that affect our moods and what we can do to support a well-balanced biochemistry

1. **Low norepinephrine and dopamine levels**
   This is associated with depression, lethargy, the inability to focus, mental fuzziness, negativity and mood disorders.

   What to do:
   - Avoid simple carbohydrates like bread, pasta, cakes, candy and ANYTHING THAT CONTAINS SUGAR (fruit sugar and honey are healthy complex carbs).

   - People who are addicted to sugar, cakes, candies, etc. are often deficient in trace minerals. If you take a teaspoon of **kelp** powder (a sea vegetable), often the craving for sugar disappears.

   - For those who eat cottage cheese, the Budwig Protocol first thing in the morning aims to balance fat metabolism. It may also be helpful for diabetics and those with cancer. Once again, sugar cravings often magically disappear when doing the Budwig Protocol. *See ResonanceRepatterning.net > BLOG* for the archived article on the Budwig Protocol.

   - For low norepinephrine and dopamine levels, try taking easily digested plant-protein snacks:

     Small amounts of raw organic unsalted sunflower seeds, pumpkin seeds, flax seeds, sesame seeds and hemp seeds; a few raw unsalted brazil nuts, walnuts, macadamia nuts, pecans or almonds (best to soak nuts and seeds for up to eight hours); kale and spinach; Hawaiian spirulina and chlorella. All of these are excellent plant-based protein snacks that are easily digested in small quantities. Try grinding a handful of seeds and adding a little organic honey, carob powder and coconut oil. Roll into balls.

In addition, whole organic raw almonds, brazil nuts, pecans, sesame seeds and pumpkin seeds are a good source of the amino acid phenylalamine, which is converted to tyrosine and then into dopamine – low levels of which are associated with depression.

- Bee pollen is one of the great foods: Dr. G.J. Binding, M.B.E., a British scientist, author and expert on nutrition, says that fresh bee pollen "contains the richest source yet revealed of vitamins, minerals, proteins, amino acids, hormones, enzymes and fats."

  Gram for gram, pollen contains 5–7 times more protein than meat, eggs or cheese, in a predigested form. It contains natural antibiotics and reverses the aging of the skin. It is excellent to take pollen daily – just a few grains or a teaspoon – as a complete source of protein, minerals, vitamins, good fats and enzymes.

2. Dopamine

Low dopamine levels are associated with a lack of motivation and poor attention span. Excess dopamine leads to an A-type personality: driven, anxious, wired, working excessively, with no ability to relax.

What to do:
- Vitamin B6 and magnesium (in the form of magnesium chloride oil on the skin or as liquid ionic magnesium chloride) prevent loss of dopamine from the brain. When given to autistic children, they start interacting with their parents.

  A deficiency of B6 leads to a depletion of dopamine and serotonin. And without vitamin B6, lactic acid becomes elevated, which leads to anxiety.

  Natural vegetarian sources of B6 (plus B1, 2, 3, 5 and 9): organic romaine lettuce, broccoli, spinach and bee pollen. *See drcarolyndean. com for B vitamin supplement or order through Amazon.*

3. **Serotonin**
    This biochemical is involved in mood control and the ability to shift one's attention. Low serotonin is associated with worry, moodiness and irritability.

    What to do:

    *   B vitamins, essential for the functioning of the brain and nervous system, decrease moodiness and depression. Romaine lettuce, broccoli, spinach, cantaloupe, berries and seeds – all raw and organic– contain B vitamins and for an excellent vitamin B supplement check Dr. Carolyn Dean's ReAlign food-based vitamin B complex. *See drcarolyndean.com*

    *   Blend various dark green vegetables like a little parsley, cilantro and spinach with a grapefruit (or a banana, apple or pear), plus a glass of water. The green smoothie, organic only, is excellent for lifting your mood and rejuvenating your energy.

    *   Vitamin B12 is good for depression and post-traumatic stress. B12 is produced by bacteria in organic, healthy soil. It is found on the surface of vegetables grown organically. It is created in a healthy intestinal tract and is reabsorbed from bile.

        B12 is lost in cooking – therefore meat, although high in B12, doesn't necessarily provide this nutrient. A reliable source is from sea vegetables: alaria (one portion provides ten times the daily amount needed), and laver, kelp, dulse, spirulina and blue-green algae. *(Contact Maine Sea Vegetables for organic high quality bulk sea vegetables: 207-565-2007.)*

    *   The precursor to serotonin is the amino acid tryptophan, which is low in depressed people. Meat and fish lose much of their tryptophan in the cooking process, or it is corrupted through heat.

    *   The herb St. John's Wort is known to enhance serotonin. Seventy percent of German physicians treat depression and anxiety with St. John's Wort.

An article in the British Medical Journal researched 1757 patients and found St. John's Wort superior to placebos and as effective as standard anti-depressant drugs, but without their side effects. (Caution: do not take St. John's Wort if you are on anti-depressant drugs.)

4. **Histamine**
Histamine stimulates the release of dopamine and serotonin.
- Excess histamine can lead to compulsive obsessive behavior: the person is driven, has high energy and often has on-going depression.

  The amino acid methionine safely lowers high histamine levels. Vegetarian sources are unsalted organic pumpkin seeds, sesame seeds and lentils (good to sprout lentils by soaking in water overnight).

- Low histamine levels may show up with any of the following signs: excess fat in lower extremities – pear-shaped figure – grand plans that are easily frustrated, hear voices inside the head, ringing in the ears, paranoia, hallucinations, need at least eight hours of sleep, mouth is usually dry, bouts of crying, tend to despair, irritability, doesn't experience pain.

What to do:
- Avoid sugar, white flour and junk foods, caffeine, colas and alcohol.

- Have a good night's sleep.

- Eat small amounts of plant-protein daily: raw organic sunflower, sesame and pumpkin seeds (preferably soaked overnight), a handful of walnuts, a few brazil nuts or almonds with fresh green organic vegetables.

5. **Melatonin**
This hormone is secreted by the pineal gland. It regulates the sleep-wake cycle. When deficient, physical and mental disabilities may result.

Animals with high melatonin levels live 30% longer and maintain their youthful appearance into old age. It has been called the fountain of youth hormone. Melatonin protects DNA, regulates sleep and buffers the build-up of stress hormones so we stay calm.

Melatonin is produced in the retina of the eyes, the pineal gland and the small intestines.

What to do
- Vigorous exercise normalizes melatonin production in the brain and allows the amino acid tryptophan to cross the brain-blood barrier and enter the brain. Vitamin D3, produced from being in direct or indirect sunlight for about 15–30 minutes daily, plus melatonin, changes moods and is beneficial for irritability and depression from sleep deprivation.

- Dr. Philpott, who carried out more than 25 years of research on negative north pole magnets, found they increase melatonin levels. He discovered that using the negative north pole ceramic block magnet on the back of the head or over the intestines, or wearing the north pole eye mask magnet, increases melatonin levels. *See ResonanceRepatterning.net > Store for negative north pole magnets*

6. **Magnesium chloride for the heart**
   Magnesium has been called the lamp of life as it is one of the most important keys to overall health and freedom from depression. The National Institute of Health (NIH) listed depression as a sign of magnesium deficiency. It was found that longterm stress-induced depression often results when magnesium levels are dangerously low. Stress depletes cellular magnesium stores.
   - Signs of magnesium deficiency in relation to depression include being withdrawn, apathetic, nervous, having tremors, muscle tension, bi-polar disorder, schizophrenia and depression.

- Magnesium chloride is the most effective form of magnesium. *See drcarolyndean.com* and Amazon, for the ionic form of magnesium chloride that is assimilated at the cellular level. You may also want to rub magnesium chloride oil into the skin. *See ancientminerals.com* for one of the best sources of magnesium chloride oil from the Zechstein Sea – a geological formation that is 250 million years old and protected from pollution at a depth of 1600–2000 meters beneath the earth's surface. Also *see resonancerepatterning.net > BLOG* for the archived article on magnesium chloride.

- Research has shown that magnesium relaxes the heart and normalizes the heartbeat – among numerous other benefits.

- Natural sources of magnesium: organic leafy greens, seeds, almonds, black-eyed peas, avocados, apples, bee pollen, beetroot, dates, dulse, kelp, figs, garlic, grapefruit.

Thirteen ways for handling depression naturally

1. **Resonance Repatterning** I have known people who have freed themselves from depression of twenty years standing by doing Resonance Repatterning on themselves and by receiving sessions – without taking drugs or supplements to change their biochemistry.

    When frequencies are in sync, biochemistry clearly changes – otherwise how could their depression lift? This is not about doing a specific Repatterning. What is most beneficial is identifying and transforming out-of-sync frequencies, and changing our resonance with negative beliefs and feelings that repetitively fire stress pathways in the brain and body.

2. **Language** The thoughts we have and the words we use activate biochemicals that match our thoughts and words. Negative words depress the system. The Negative Thoughts Repatterning (from the Transforming Unconscious Patterns book) is an excellent resource for negative language or thoughts. A practitioner used this Repatterning after the 2017 earthquake in Mexico City for people who couldn't sleep, were terrified, found themselves

trembling uncontrollably and couldn't eat. She reported that after doing the Negative Thoughts Repatterning their symptoms cleared up.

A dramatic example from my early days of teaching Resonance Repatterning was a lady who attended one of my seminars. She was seriously depressed: she never smiled, she sat by herself, didn't talk to anyone and there was nothing I could do to create a connection with her.

However, on the second day she came in full of energy. She told the whole group that she was 38 years old and lived with her parents because she was so depressed she couldn't get a job. She had insomnia – hadn't had a full night's sleep in about eight years and she had pain all over her body – also for many years.

During the seminar the previous day I had demonstrated the power of the Zip-Ups Energizing Option – zipping yourself up by running your hand up the front midline of your body about an inch from the body. The Zip-Ups Energizing Option strengthens the acupuncture Conception Vessel – a reservoir of energy for the six Yin Meridians. I explained and demonstrated that whenever we hear or see anything negative we can maintain our energy by doing the Zip-Ups.

The lady told us that she had never heard a single positive word from either of her parents. Everything they said was negative. So she went home after the seminar and spent every minute 'zipping' herself up in response to everything they said.

The next day she woke up and thought, "Something is wrong." Then she suddenly realized that she had no pain and that she had slept throughout the whole night. She said, "I feel so happy I could dance in front of all of you!" An amazing transformation from the day before. Clearly her biochemistry had changed!

This example is an important reminder for all of us concerning the power of language – our own and others' – to strengthen or weaken our field and the field of others, and to cause biochemicals of depression to manifest.

Remember, we heard 'No' and 'Don't' once every nine minutes as infants and children. Words are energy frequencies and we need to be conscious of the energy-words we are projecting.

The thoughts we have are directly related to the kind of food we eat. Observe for yourself how you feel and think when you eat fresh organic fruit and greens, seeds and a few nuts. Then observe what happens to your mood and energy in the hours after you eat sugar, junk food, white flour, pasta, alcohol, caffeine and colas, etc.

And remember the language of gratitude: it is said that you can't be grateful and depressed at the same time!

3. **Movement** Our chi life energy must move. When our energy is sluggish we get depressed, and sick too. The trouble is that when we are depressed the last thing we want to do is move.

There are many endorphin receptors in the deep limbic brain, which control our feelings and mood.

Exercise that we **enjoy** releases endorphins, which give us a sense of well-being and pleasure.

Exercise increases blood flow throughout the brain, which is why Dr. Amen prescribes strenuous exercise for his depressed patients.

Exercise also normalizes melatonin production in the brain and allows the amino acid tryptophan to cross the brain-blood barrier and enter the brain. Tryptophan is the precursor to serotonin, which is low in depressed people.

Exercise done with anger or dislike has little benefit. Only exercise done with enjoyment gives positive benefits. So move in the way you love: dancing, yoga, tai chi, walking, bouncing on a rebounder, lifting weights. Try walking with a bounce in your step when you feel moody or depressed and see what happens!

4. **Breathing** Many brain problems are caused by an imbalance of oxygen and carbon dioxide. The brain needs most of the oxygen we breathe, in order to function – more than any other tissue or organ in the body.

   Try the Anulom Breath – breathing in the left nostril and out of the right nostril – for ten minutes in the morning and ten minutes in the evening. It clears your energy channels, calms your mind and releases negative thoughts.

   Perhaps one of the most powerful breaths is the Buteyko "Control Pause" breath, which balances carbon dioxide and oxygen levels. In Russia, this Buteyko Control Pause breath was originally used for curing asthma, emphysema and bronchial disorders, but has been found to be an essential health tool for everyone. See Teresa Hale *Breathing Free* for in-depth information, Patrick McKeown's excellent book, *The Oxygen Advantage* and SPIRAL UP! by Chloe Wordsworth for the Buteyko breath **How To.**

5. **Sunlight** Lack of full spectrum light is associated with depression. Research has proven that we need 30–50 minutes of direct or indirect full spectrum light a day. Glasses, dark glasses, contacts and windows block the reception of full spectrum sunlight, preventing it from entering our eyes and brain.

   Dr. John Ott, the great light researcher, reported that four women who were unable to get pregnant succeeded in getting pregnant when they gave up wearing their dark glasses and received a daily dose of full-spectrum sunlight. Light works with a form of Vitamin D3 and melatonin to generate changes in mood. Dr. Krudsen reports 165 diseases treated with UV light.

6. **Negative north pole magnets** These magnets have been shown to increase melatonin production. *See resonancerepatterning.net >STORE*

7. **Good fats** Many people are deficient in the good fats: the omega-3s from natural plant sources like chia and flaxseeds. One teaspoon of organic chia seeds every day rejuvenates your energy and makes you feel great! The Native Americans would take chia before a long day of strenuous walking and running.

Flaxseeds and/or chia ground up and mixed with fruit and vegetables in a blender makes an energy drink that takes only a minute to make. Soaking them overnight first (to release the enormous energy of the sprouting seed and eliminate phytic acid) and blending them into your smoothie makes a power-house drink!

The Budwig Protocol – four tablespoons of organic cottage cheese and two tablespoons of **organic** flaxseed oil (make sure the flaxseed oil you buy is dated, freshly-pressed, organic and refrigerated) provides the omega-3 fats needed for balancing fat metabolism, cancer-prevention and re-energizing the brain. Blend with a banana and **organic** berries like blueberries and strawberries (must be organic as non-organic berries are the most heavily sprayed with insecticides).

8. **Colon cleanse** Many people are depressed because their colon is filled with toxic material, even if they go to the bathroom daily! Few people realize they are carrying around ten pounds or more of fecal matter in their colon from the toxic residues they are not eliminating, which also provides a fertile ground for parasites.

   Phone 1-800-herbdoc for information and newsletters on Dr. Schulze's organic herbal colon cleanse, liver detox and much more. Dr. Schulze is a naturopath and herbalist who is dedicated to people being well and has brought many people back from death's door from every known disease.

9. **Bach Flower Remedies** Put one drop of the mother tincture in a glass of water and sip all day:

   • **Rock Rose**: Extreme fear and panic.

   • **Mimulus**: Worried and fearful about what is known to you.

   • **Cherry Plum**: Loss of mental control; temper; fear you will hurt yourself or others.

- **Aspen**: Foreboding; vague fears and apprehension.

- **Red Chestnut**: Over-caring; fears worse for loved ones.

- **Gentian**: Despondent, discouraged, dejected for a known cause.

- **Gorse**: Extreme hopelessness; despair; pessimism; 'what's the use'.

- **Honeysuckle**: Nostalgia; live in the past.

- **Wild Rose**: Resignation; apathy; no ambition.

- **Olive**: Complete exhaustion; drained of energy.

- **Mustard**: Deep gloom; melancholia; dark cloud comes and goes for no reason.

- **Larch**: Anticipation of failure; feel inferior; no confidence.

- **Agrimony**: Inner torture is hidden behind a façade of cheerfulness.

- **Centaury**: Doormat; exploited; can't say no; over-anxious to please.

- **Walnut**: Transitions and new surroundings bring fear.

- **Holly**: Lack of love; envy; jealousy; hatred; suspicion.

- **Crab Apple**: Feel unclean in mind and body; self-dislike; disgust; cleansing remedy.

- **Oak**: Strong and courageous but unable to struggle any more against illness and adversity.

- **Willow**: Resentment; bitterness; poor me.

- **Star of Bethlehem**: Fright; trauma; great sorrow.

- **Sweet Chestnut**: Anguish; desolation; reached the limit of endurance, but not suicidal.

10. **Laughter** Produces endorphins of joy that boost your immune system and immediately makes you feel better. Watch funny movies; do the Laughter Breath daily (Ha-Ha-Ha's with exaggerated belly laughing movements) to get your laughter nutrient.

11. **Balance your Five Elements**
    a. **Wood**: Find your vision – it gives your life meaning and gives you a sense of self-esteem. Go into action to reach a goal, to stand for something right. Channel anger into a creative outlet.

    b. **Fire**: Be with friends. Create connections of the heart. Do activities, not for the sake of the activity, but to enjoy relating and connecting. Go to a park and enjoy watching people and talking to people. Have fun. Laugh.

    c. **Earth**: Equilibrium between being in your center and moving your energy out into the world to nurture others. Tai Chi; Chi Kung. Practice self-acceptance at every opportunity. Enjoy giving. Enjoy receiving.

    d. **Metal**: Breathing; colon cleanse; spiritual practice; meditation; appreciate yourself; self-acceptance: value each thing you have done, rather than devalue yourself and complain about what you have **not** done.

    e. **Water**: Movement; explore and do those things that make you feel energized and powerful. Recharge your energy with sleep. Enjoy relaxing and listening. Use your energy for your spiritual practice and to manifest your life purpose.

12. **Magnesium chloride oil** Massage the oil into any part of your body. *p.157*

13. Read ***Depression-Free Naturally*** by Joan Mathews Larson Ph.D.

FURTHER READING

Victoria Boutenko. *Green for Life.*

Joseph Chilton Pierce. *The Biology of Transcendence.*

Gabriel Cousens, MD. *Conscious Eating.*

Teresa Hale. *Breathing free: the 5-day breathing programme that will change your life.*

Joan Mathews Larson. *Depression-Free Naturally.*

Patrick McKeown. *The Oxygen Advantage: the simple, scientifically proven breathing techniques for a healthier, slimmer, faster, and fitter you.*

Rachel Naomi Remen, MD. *Kitchen Table Wisdom.*

5. DEPRESSED HEART REPATTERNING

This session focuses on what keeps us depressed and firing neural pathways that create anxiety, depression and mood swings.

Depression is an issue that usually needs a number of sessions – muscle checking from any of the twelve Resonance Repatterning manuals for what you may need in each session.

There has never been a specific Repatterning protocol just for depression. So the Depression Repatterning needs to be used in the context of a series of sessions that will call for various Repatterning protocols as the client's system reveals its own unique needs.

A. Name the depression

Ask, "In what way do you feel depressed – how does your depression show up for you?" *[cr] *(will be on/umb on because client resonates with the out-of-sync frequencies causing the depression)*.

Deeper understanding in relation to the survival brain

A negative experience of any sort – whether outside yourself or in your own thoughts and feelings and how you react to your experiences – automatically and unconsciously shifts your energy from your higher pre-frontal cortex (behind your brow) to your lower reptilian survival brain in the back of your head and your emotionally reactive limbic brain. This shift locks your higher brain into the service of your lower and emotionally reactive survival brains. This makes understanding, clear thinking and inner harmony difficult or impossible.

B. Identify the primary conflict in relation to depression

Do {a–i} in sequence.

Explain, "Our primary caregivers are usually our mother and father plus our sibling relationships. As an infant or child when we felt judged and not accepted, or we were neglected, punished or abused, we closed down our spontaneous, open, expanded life-energy and moved into constriction and shame. We disconnect from the oneness of all life and our heart and feel separated and isolated. Healing begins as we change our resonance with the early stress and conflict that the ones we need and love are also part of our pain when we closed our heart.

a. **Read the story of the Senoi and the Yequana** *p.138*
   Ask, "What does this story mean for you?" *[cr] with "I (*name the positive meaning*)" (*will be off/umb off*).

b. **The mother modeling**
   Ask, "What was negative about what your mother modeled for you?" *[cr] (*will be on/umb on because client still resonates with the broken bond with the mother*).

c. **Mother bonding**
   Ask, "Which bonding ways were missing for you in relation to your mother: breast feeding, eye-gazing, hearing your mother's voice, having the smell of your mother's fragrance, or touch and holding fairly continuously in the first nine months of your life? *[cr] with "(*Name the missing bonding actions*) are missing with my mother and this still creates a bonding stress for me in the present" (*will be on/umb on*).

d. **The father modeling**
   Ask, "What was negative about your relationship bond with your father? What did he model in his relationship with you that was less than ideal?" *[cr] (*will be on/umb on because client still resonates with the broken bond with the father*).

e. **Lack of perceived acceptance**
   Ask, "How did you feel unaccepted or unacceptable in relation to your mother or father?" *[cr] with "I continue to feel unacceptable because (*name what is not accepted*)" (*will be on/umb on*).

f. *Ask*, "Do you see how this pattern negatively influences or is repeated in your adult relationships – particularly your intimate partnerships? How?" *[cr] (*will be on/umb on*).

Explain: Every time we think about our negative past, or repeat the same negative pattern in the present, we re-enforce the same brain-body neural pathways, which then become hardwired and automatic. What in the past might have been a *path*way, now becomes a *high*way. In this way we re-activate problems and pain from our past, which are superimposed on our present relationships and repeated in the patterns of our life.

g. **The feeling**
Ask, "How do you imagine you felt in response to your parents not giving you the unconditional love, bonding and acceptance you needed as an infant?" *[cr] with "I continue to feel (*name the feeling*) in the present" *(will be on/umb on because client resonates with this negative feeling stress response).*

h. **The belief**
Ask, "What do you imagine you believed about yourself or others as a result of not receiving the unconditional love, bonding and acceptance you needed as an infant?" *[cr] *(will be on/umb on because client resonates with this stressed thought as though it is true).*

i. **The memory**
Ask, "What memory do you have when you were forced to separate from your mother – when you were unable to separate from her when you wanted to?" *[cr] *(will be on/umb on).*

j. **What Client wants instead**
Explain: Your experience is in your mind. And the negative image you resonate with is still activating stress neural pathways in the present.

However, a positive vision you resonate with creates new neural pathways. Once the pathways of your positive vision are well established, the the old pathways will atrophy from lack of use and will no longer control your relationships and how you respond to life.

"What new and positive vision do you want in relation to bonding with your mother and father and a positive separation from them, instead of these old images?" *[cr] *(will be off/umb off because client does not resonate with this new positive vision of bonding).*

C. Name the heart disconnection that resulted as client's energy constricted

(**mcs**) {a–e} for the one(s) needed and then do {f}.

a. *[cr] with "I feel isolated and alone" *(will be on/umb on because client resonates with this earlier stress response of loneliness as though it is still present).*

b. *[cr] with "I live in fear of losing the bond of love" *(will be on/umb on because client resonates with this earlier stress response of fear as though it is still present).*

c. *[cr] with "I feel ashamed that my (mother • father) withdraws her/his love because I am unacceptable as I am and I don't please her/him" *(will be on/umb on because client resonates with this earlier stress response of shame as though it is still present).*

d. *[cr] with "(I doubt myself • I can't accept myself as a whole being • My body is unacceptable • I feel separate from others • I am unacceptable)" *(will be on/umb on because client resonates with this earlier stress response of separation from self as though it is still present).*

e. *[cr] with "I can no longer explore life and my relationships with total involvement, focus, joy, spontaneity and forgetfulness of self" *(will be on/umb on because client resonates with this earlier inhibiting response as though it is still present).*

f. **Identify the language that keeps you stuck in your old stress neural pathways**
Ask, "What do you dislike about yourself?" *[cr] with "I am (*Name the dislike items, but leave out the words 'I dislike'*)" (will be on/umb on because client resonates with this negative self-talk).*

Understanding of the power of language to activate stress neural pathways and feelings
Ask, "If you said these dislike things about a friend, what kind of friendship would you have? When we think about ourselves in these negative ways, it's natural that we get depressed because we are no longer treating ourselves as a friend!"

D. **Identify the Five Element imbalance that depresses the heart**
(**mcs**) {a–e} for the primary Element(s) involved.
a. (**mcs**) **The Wood Elementis involved?** (**mcs**) {1–8}. *[cr] (will be on/ umb on).*
   1. I feel pessimistic about myself and the possibility for a new beginning.
   2. I judge myself in a negative light, no matter how good I am.
   3. I judge others in a negative light.
   4. I feel hopeless and angry.
   5. I can't envision any positive options.
   6. My growth and potential are stunted.
   7. I lose my self-confidence.
   8. I don't go into action (to create positive change • for what I want).

b. (**mcs**) **The Fire Element involved?** (**mcs**) {1–9}. *[cr] (will be on/ umb on).*
   1. I have lost my joy in life.
   2. I can't receive love through eye-gazing.
   3. (I avoid eye contact • I can't maintain eye contact so I turn away)
   4. I can't connect from my heart or feel another's heart connection.
   5. I feel confused and can't sort out who to bond with.

6. I feel threatened by close bonding and love.
7. Others feel threatened by close bonding and love with me.
8. I have lost my sense of excitement.
9. (I feel as though I have no friends • I don't open my heart to friendship • I don't take the time to do things with others).

c. **(mcs) The Earth Element involved?** (mcs) {1–6}. *[cr] *(will be on/ umb on).*
   1. I feel anxious about bonding and closeness.
   2. I need to take care of everyone's needs to avoid their displeasure.
   3. (Others/*name person*) doesn't takes care of my needs or nurture me.
   4. I have lost my center of equilibrium and my mind is scattered.
   5. I feel locked within myself, unable to move outwards into the world with ease and contentment.
   6. If I am generous (I want something in return • I want to be liked and loved as a result of my giving).

d. **(mcs) The Metal Element involve?** (mcs) {1–8}. *[cr] *(will be on/ umb on).*
   1. I have disconnected from my spirit / my authentic self.
   2. (I have no value • I am worthless).
   3. I never feel good enough.
   4. I disrespect others and diminish them as a way to feel better about myself.
   5. I put others on a pedestal in the hope that they will value me.
   6. The Divine does not accept and love me as I am. I will never be good enough.
   7. I feel like a hermit, cut off from relationship with others and life
   8. I have lost sight of my values.

e. **(mcs) The Water Element involved?** (mcs) {1–8}. *[cr] *(will be on/ umb on).*
   1. I am exhausted.
   2. I can't move freely.
   3. I feel powerless in my relationship to (*name person*).

4. I do not use my willpower to (move forward • manifest my potential and spiritual purpose).
5. I feel afraid and constricted.
6. I have disconnected from my essential self.
7. I don't listen to (my inner knowing / others).
8. I am not using my energy to manifest my life purpose.

E. Identify the Element balance needed to uplift the heart
(**mcs**) for the primary Element(s) needed for healing and wholeness.

a. (mcs) The Wood Element is needed? (**mcs**) {1–7}. *[**cr**] *(will be off/ umb off)*.

1. I am optimistic and full of hope.
2. I transform my judgments into acceptance and benevolence.
3. I see what is interesting and positive in others.
4. I forgive.
5. I see what I want and go into action to manifest it.
6. I love growing, learning and changing.
7. I am tolerant of others' differences.

b. (mcs) The Fire Element is needed? (**mcs**) {1–6}. *[**cr**] *(will be on/ umb on)*.

1. I am filled with joy in the divine play of life.
2. I receive and give love through loving warm eye contact.
3. I know in my heart who is trustworthy for me to bond closely with.
4. My love relationships are reciprocal.
5. I always keep the lines of communication open.
6. (I am open to communicating with others • I am interested in others' lives, with what excites and inspires them and in their creative interests).

c. (mcs) The Earth Element is needed? (**mcs**) {1–5}. *[**cr**] *(will be off/ umb off)*.

1. I live from my center.
2. I trust that all my needs are taken care of.

3. (I am giving • I am generous from my heart).
4. I love supporting others in having their needs met.
5. (I have a sense of belonging • I belong in my family and in this world).

d. **(mcs) The Metal Element is needed?** (mcs) {1–5}. *[cr] *(will be off/ umb off)*.
   1. I live from my authentic self.
   2. I am connected to the Divine within myself – my rock of self-confidence and my ultimate value.
   3. I am good enough.
   4. I respect all beings and appreciate the Divine within myself and within each person I meet.
   5. I am loved by the Divine.

e. **(mcs) The Water Element is needed?** (mcs) {1–6}. *[cr] *(will be off/ umb off)*.
   1. I am full of energy and ready to go, nothing is held back.
   2. I flow according to where (Nature/the Divine/my destiny) leads me.
   3. I use my willpower to manifest my spiritual potential.
   4. I transcend my fears and live courageously.
   5. I stay in touch with my essential self.
   6. I am a listening presence to (my own inner knowing and wisdom / others).

F. Reconnecting to the 'Senoi' within
(mcs) {a–p} for the one(s) needed. *[cr] *(will be off/umb off)*.
a. My *(name the age)* child aspect is totally loved and accepted just as I am.
b. I am free of shame.
c. I am free of fear.
d. I am free to explore my world and also to bond with love.
e. I trust myself.
f. I am good enough.
g. I am part of the divine play of love and learning.
h. I say Yes to life and love and express my essence, which is love in action.

i. I am a whole.

j. I find wonderful models for how to be and grow in this world.

k. I am free of judging myself and others.

l. I let go of others' judgments about me, understanding that their judgments are their problem.

m. I go into appropriate well-thought-out actions according to each situation.

n. I avoid hurting others.

o. I am pleasant to all people.

p. I avoid trying to influence/coerce others to do what I want them to do.

G. Identify the birth note Energizing Option needed

a. Identify the client's four birth notes *p.25* and (**mcs**) if the mother's or father's birth notes are needed. If one of the client's notes coincides with one of the mother's or father's birth notes, this may be the note needed. (**mcs**) for details.

b. Client needs to read the six biochemicals that may affect his/her moods and heart? *p.73* Client can decide if he/she feels one of these options could be important.

c. Resonance Repatterning practitioners will now recheck the *[**cr**] statements and confirm any change in resonance.

H. After completing the Energizing Option

(**mcs**) Client needs a positive action from the 13 ways to transform depression? *p.158* (**mcs**) for details on which one, and talk it over to make sure client wants to do the action.

HOW TO USE THE DEPRESSED HEART REPATTERNING IN YOUR DAILY LIFE EVEN IF YOU HAVE NOT YET ATTENDED A RESONANCE REPATTERNING SEMINAR

- Start putting into action one or more of the fourteen ways to transform depression. Start with whatever feels right to you. Observe the effect it has on your anxiety, stress, self-doubt, anger, fear and depression. Any positive change lets you know you are going in the right direction.

- Read through the section on your biochemistry. Start eating foods that support a balanced biochemistry. Observe if you begin to lose an interest in junk foods, sugar, flour products, colas, coffee and alcohol.

- Take one or two parts of the Depression Repatterning and do an Energizing Option to change your resonance.

- With depression you may want to seriously consider having Resonance Repatterning sessions from a certified practitioner and make sure you have whatever therapeutic support you need.

- Start changing your thought habits – every time you go into negative thinking, get up and move, laugh or change the negative thinking into acceptance and gratitude.

RR SESSIONS: If you would like to receive the complete Repatterning with a professional Resonance Repatterning Practitioner, in person or over the phone, go to ResonanceRepatterning.net > Sessions for RR Institute Practitioners worldwide who have listed themselves on the RRI website.

RR SEMINARS: If you would like to attend Resonance Repatterning seminars in person or online, so you can use RR effectively on yourself and/or others, go to ResonanceRepatterning.net > Seminars for the list of teachers endorsed by the Resonance Repatterning Institute to teach.

6. TRIANGLES OF THE HEART

Becoming human means discovering our fullness and learning to live from it. This involves bringing forth more of who we really are and becoming more available to whatever life presents.

John Welwood, Ph.D., *Journey of the Heart*

Triangles in relationship have nothing to do with threesome relationships.

Triangles – whether coherent or non-coherent – are a state of mind that we act out in our relationships.

The three points of the triangle represent the three roles or ways of being that we play out in our relationships.

When our triangle is non-coherent, playing any of these three roles damages us and our relationships.

When our triangle is coherent, we live from three ways of being that support our growth and lead to the fulfillment of the inherent needs we all want to experience in our relationships: security, happiness, achievement, love and meaning.

The non-coherent triangle

When our relationships become derailed in small or big ways, we know that we are acting out one or more non-coherent roles – represented by the three points of the triangle. Often we switch from one role to another – sometimes at high speed.

As long as we are stuck in any of these non-coherent roles, we won't get our basic needs met for security, happiness, achievement, love and meaning in our relationships. And we'll miss out on what is possible in our relationships – to live with an open and loving heart.

The three points of the triangle

The three points of the triangle are represented as *the perpetrator, the victim* and *the fix-it savior.*

We may start out feeling like a victim when someone does or says something that upsets or hurts us. Then if we complain about this person, get reactive, critical, make them wrong or go into negative actions, we now move into the perpetrator role. And the original perpetrator is now the victim.

If we are driven to fix challenging situations – trying out one solution after another to lower our own level of discomfort, attempting to get others to follow our advice and solutions, we are now in the fix-it savior role.

And when our solutions are ignored or rejected, we may jump into the victim role, or if we get reactive and defensive, we may jump into the perpetrator role.

So the pattern keeps repeating itself. We can spend our life shifting from one of these non-coherent roles to another whenever we face a difficult challenge in relationship.

As long as we resonate with one or more of these three roles, we will be unable to experience a deeper understanding of ourselves and the other person involved. Our relationship challenges hold the potential for us to realize more love, appreciation and pleasure in our relationships. Stuck in the non-coherent triangle, we undermine this realization.

If we think honestly about any difficulty in our relationships, what do we see ourselves as? The victim? The perpetrator? Or the savior, helplessly coming up with advice and solutions that never resolve the underlying difficulty?

The coherent triangle

So what is the answer? The coherent triangle offers a new way to resolve our relationship upsets without having to go into the non-coherent triangle at all.

When our relationships work well:
- we feel connected to the other person

- we are energized by the relationship

- there is mutual respect

- we trust that we can share the truth of who we are, free of being judged

- we trust that the other person won't talk negatively about us either in person or behind our back

- we feel safe in the relationship, that we won't be hurt

- we have faith that the other person has our best interest at heart, as we have their best interest at heart

- we know that when inevitable miscommunications or upsets occur, we will mutually share our different points of view, be heard and understood free of defensiveness and reactivity

- even when the two different perceptions are not resolved, we are able to sustain the bond of love and trust

In this type of relationship the three points of the coherent triangle are occupied by three different ways of being.

The open-hearted hero instead of the victim

In the coherent triangle, instead of the victim, we have the open-hearted hero who responds from the heart rather than from a sympathetic nervous system (SNS) fear response that makes us defensive or takes us into denial, low self-confidence, helplessness and a feeling of weakness. The open-hearted hero keeps his or her heart open to love and communication regardless of others' negative or even abusive words and actions.

The noble adversary instead of the perpetrator

When we realize there is no accident in what is happening to us, we stop discharging anger, blame and criticism onto others. In this way our perpetrator is transformed into the noble adversary.

The noble adversary within us wants us to take the high road in every challenging situation. The noble adversary insists that we grow, that we respond positively to the problem, that we raise our consciousness and realize our higher potential as a human being.

The noble adversary understands through acceptance that every negative situation is a reflection of some pattern from within ourselves and from our own past. This pattern emerges in the form of upsets and difficulties. The upset, whatever it is, is a messenger bringing our own pattern to our notice. With awareness, and a shift in resonance, resolution and growth are possible.

We could also say that the upset itself is our noble adversary, demanding coherent transformation in us, self-mastery over some internal weakness, and an honest healing response rather than an undermining reactive response.

As noble adversaries, we transform a negative situation into one that results in growth, learning, a new understanding and appreciation of each other and a deepening bond of trust in the relationship.

The wise teacher and friend instead of the fix-it savior

Instead of the fix-it savior trying to mask the underlying issues with solutions and advice, we have the wise teacher who is our friend. The wise teacher is one who:

- has something important to impart to us that will further our inner transformation

- models for us how to listen free of judgment

- is fully present, undistracted

- shares his or her truth, wisdom and insights in a way that helps us change our angle of vision

Seeing a difficult situation from the point of view of the coherent triangle, we naturally gain a deeper understanding of our self and our situation.

Resonating with the coherent triangle

When we resonate with these three coherent ways of being, we consciously enjoy open-hearted relationships.

Rather than seeing someone as a perpetrator, we treat someone who is difficult for us as a noble adversary who has an important lesson we need to learn. Instead of reacting with anger, we ourselves become noble adversaries who courageously bring issues to the surface to be handled and transformed.

When facing difficulties, we become the open-hearted hero. Instead of responding with weakness or self-pity, we are self-empowered, standing firm in our self-confidence. In this way we lovingly and respectfully speak our truth and model our truth, and go into right action with strength and courage.

And in the face of challenging situations – instead of lowering our level of discomfort by giving easy advice and solutions, we become the wise teacher and friend for others, living a higher state of being in action. We find meaning in every circumstance. We see the patterns asking for self-mastery. And what we share has power because it comes from the heart of a higher understanding.

REMEMBER TO BOW

Terry Dobson relates an incident, which he saw when traveling by train through the Japanese Alps, that illustrates the coherent triangle.

There were a lot of college kids on the train on their way to a mountain climbing vacation – all with rucksacks and ice axes tied to the outside.

At one of the stops, the kids got off. One of them pulled his rucksack off the rack and the ice axe fell like a guillotine onto the head of an old man.

Terry writes, "I froze. The axe clattered to the floor. The old man woke up and clutched his head. Blood started squirting from the wound. He looked up at the kid, who was absolutely aghast. The old man saw that the boy had no idea what to do. He reached down, grabbed the ice axe, and handed it to the kid with a bow. He said, 'Have a good day. Enjoy your climb.' How is that for humility! I hope that when I get to be that age and have an ice axe in my head, I'll remember to bow."

The old man chose to be the open-hearted hero, rather than the victim. He chose to be the noble adversary, rather than the reactive angry perpetrator. He chose to be the wise teacher and friend who modeled respect, kindness and forgiveness. And his response, his story, continues to be a gift of higher learning for all of us.

If doing the Repatterning, return to {D} p.190

Another story has a different learning for us about the transformation our triangles offer us.

THE STORY OF FIVE IMPORTANT WORDS

Once upon a time there was a king who had a beautiful ring. Hidden inside the ring was a tiny container. The king wanted to put something in this container that would bring him wisdom and a deeper understanding of himself and life. So he called all the court's philosophers together and told them to write five important words to place inside his ring. But nothing they wrote satisfied him.

Finally his trusted servant, the son of a wise man, told the king that many years ago his father had inscribed five words on a tiny piece of paper and had told him that one day he would place this paper inside the king's ring. But there was one condition: the trusted servant told his king, "I can only give you these five words if you promise to read them only in your moment of direst need." The king promised and his servant placed the words inside the ring.

Some time later the king's country was attacked. The opposing army was strong and the king was forced to run from the battlefield with his enemies in pursuit. Fleeing for his life, he came to a fork in the path before him. He hesitated for a moment before galloping down the right-hand way only to find to his dismay that the path ended at an abyss. He now realized that his death was immanent: his enemies were behind him and the abyss was before him.

Then he remembered the five words inside his ring, only to be read in his moment of direst need. He opened the ring and took out the words that were beautifully inscribed on the tiny piece of parchment. He read: "AND THIS TOO SHALL PASS." Immediately he was filled with peace of mind: he felt only love for all beings – enemies and friends alike. He stood quietly with inner stillness of mind and heart, in a state of great inner joy. After some hours he realized that his enemies must have taken the left-hand fork in the path – and his life was saved.

The king managed to get back to his kingdom where he created law and order and re-built a strong army to protect his people from harm.

Some years later his enemies decided to attack yet again, but this time the king met his enemies with strength and they were defeated.

The king now called for a general celebration. Decked in his richest clothes and seated in his golden chariot the king, with his trusted servant standing behind him, drove through the streets of his capital, enjoying the love and appreciation of the crowds, the festivities, the dancing and music.

After a while the king's trusted servant said, "It is now time for you to open your ring and read the five words once more." The king laughed and said, "Why? This isn't a time of my direst need?" The servant again said, "Please, it is time for you to read the five words once more."

So the king opened his ring and again took out the five words beautifully inscribed on the tiny piece of parchment. He read aloud, "AND THIS TOO SHALL PASS." Once more he was filled with peace of mind and deep inner stillness amidst all the noise, lost in a state of inner joy.

If doing the Repatterning, return to {F} p.191

$\sim$

A meaning in relation to triangles

One of our needs is to find meaning. So let's look at the meaning of this story in terms of the non-coherent and coherent triangles.

When the king resonated with the non-coherent triangle, he lived in a world of victim and perpetrator. His enemies were the perpetrator and he was the victim. As long as he views life through this lens, he lives in danger: the abyss before him and his enemies behind. There are no fix-it solutions when we live in the victim-perpetrator mode.

Previous to the battle, the king was searching for the five most important words. He is searching for an inner awakening of some kind – greater coherence, wisdom, peace of mind.

The king is receptive to a new way of being, and the wise teacher – who is always our trusted servant, the one who serves us by being the true friend – puts the five words in his ring: words that will give him the grace to transcend all life's challenges, whether negative or positive.

The ring symbolizes the sacred circle of divine love and harmony that is always with us through the ups and downs of life. With these five words he has the potential for a higher state of consciousness – to live from the coherent triangle even while holding the reins of power.

When he is defeated and flees for his life, facing the abyss of death, the king manifests this potential in action. His consciousness is raised, which is the only true solution. We can only transcend life's challenges by raising our consciousness and accessing the divinity within.

Realizing that all things pass, that this world of illusion has no reality, the king discovers the purpose of being human. He experiences the divine in the silence and stillness within. And in the midst of danger he knows only peace.

The king discovers his fullness – how to bring forth his spiritual being and live from it.

Now from this new place of consciousness and understanding, he rebuilds his army – the symbol of his inner strength. And this time his enemies – the perpetrator of his own weaknesses – are routed. The king is no longer a victim of his weaknesses. He is free of the non-coherent triangle.

But even amidst the celebration of this higher state of consciousness and his freedom from the lower tendencies of his mind, the wise teacher ensures that the king stays conscious, balanced, that he understands that neither the good nor the so-called bad are real and lasting.

Pain and pleasure are two sides of the same coin.

Our direst moment may be when we are up against the wall and all feels lost. Equally, our direst moment may be when we are at the pinnacle of success in the world. As the saying goes, 'Give a man power and money and you will see whether he has character.'

In both pain and pleasure, in each of these states of mind, there are lessons to be learned – lessons we can only learn if we are grounded in the coherent triangle, resonating in our heart with a higher state of consciousness.

The Triangle Repatterning

The Triangle Repatterning focuses on

- what keeps us in the non-coherent triangle of the perpetrator, victim and fix-it savior in our relationships

- how we can change our resonance with these three non-coherent roles

- how we can resonate with the three ways of being found in the coherent triangle so we stay connected to our essence – the heart of our higher consciousness

FURTHER READING

John Welwood. *Journey of the Heart.*

Terry Dobson. *It's a Lot like Dancing: An Aikido Journey.*

6. TRIANGLES OF THE HEART REPATTERNING

A. Name the situation

    a. *Ask*, "Is there a situation in your life where you feel wronged or hurt by someone?" Get the details on the situation. *[cr] with "(*Name person*) (*name the negative action or words*). I am his/her victim and he/she is my perpetrator" *(will be on/umb on because client resonates with feeling victimized by the difficult situation).*

    b. *Ask*, "How do you imagine you might be a perpetrator for (*name person*)? How do you imagine you have hurt or upset (*name person*)?" *[cr] with "When I (*name the negative actions or words*), I become (*name person*)'s perpetrator and he/she becomes the victim" *(will be on/umb on because client also resonates with being the perpetrator to the other's victim).*

    c. *Ask*, "How do you try to be the fix-it savior with (*name person/other*) – trying to make everything OK by giving advice or coming up with solutions, even though the real issue isn't addressed and resolved?" *[cr] with "I (*name what you do to try to fix the problem*) but it doesn't help" *(will be on/umb on because client resonates with being the fix-it savior).*

Understanding the non-coherent triangle

So long as you feel at the mercy of someone else's negative behavior or hurtful words, you are in the victim role and you lose your peace of mind.

So long as you blame, criticize or judge anyone, or think your are right and they are wrong, you are in the perpetrator role and you lose your peace of mind.

So long as you feel it is your responsibility to fix the other person's problems and upsets through your advice or solutions, you are in the fix-it savior role and you lose your peace of mind.

We usually resonate with at least two of the roles in the non-coherent triangle in any given situation.

B. **Name the non-coherent perpetrator, victim, fix-it savior resonance**

Do {a–c} in sequence.

a. **(mcs) victim resonance is involved?**

(mcs) {1–7}. *[cr] *(will be on/umb on)*.

1. *(Name person)* hurts me and there is nothing I can do about it.
2. I am (bad • wrong • weak • guilty • unlovable • unworthy • a failure).
3. I deserve to be punished.
4. (I blame myself • I am blamed) for what goes wrong.
5. I am the innocent victim of *(other's/name person)*'s thoughtless actions.
6. I do everything for *(name person)* to make him/her happy, but (nothing helps • He/She still criticizes and blames me • He/She still abandons me).
7. *(Name person)* doesn't love me in spite of all I do.

b. **(mcs) perpetrator resonance is involved?**

(mcs) {1–8}. *[cr] *(will be on/umb on)*.

1. I manipulate the situation (to get what I want • to prove that I am right and *(name person)* is wrong).
2. I punish the person who hurts me by (remaining silent • withdrawing my love and friendship • cutting off the relationship).
3. I react with (anger • judgments) in response to someone hurting me, even if they didn't mean to.
4. I make *(name person)* who hurts/upsets me miserable by *(name what is done)*.
5. I am right and *(name person)* is wrong.
6. I (criticize • blame • judge) *(name person)*.
7. I justify my actions and words to prove that I am right and he/she is wrong.
8. I (quarrel with • argue with • swear at • demean • disrespect • gossip about) *(name person)*.

c. **(mcs)** The fix-it savior resonance is involved?
   (mcs) {1–4}. *[cr] (will be on/umb on).
   1. I have to (make everything OK • keep the peace), even if the underlying issue is not addressed.
   2. In the face of problems, I lower my level of stress by (offering quick solutions and advice • being in denial that there is a problem • acting cheerfully as a way to by-pass the problem, but feeling anxious underneath • giving (name person) what he/she wants even if this feels wrong to me • trying to make (name person) happy).
   3. I keep giving and giving but my solutions (aren't acted on • are not appreciated • are ignored • don't create a resolution • don't create happiness in our relationship).
   4. I go into action to sort out (name person's/everyone's) problems even though (I have not been asked for advice • my advice is not taken).

C. Name the reptilian and limbic brain fight-flight response
Do {a–d} in sequence.
   a. *Ask,* "What is most threatening for you about your situation with (name person)?" *[cr] (will be on/umb on).

   b. *Ask,* "What negative feeling would you have if this threat actually happened?" *[cr] with "I feel (name the negative feeling)" (will be on/ umb on).

   c. *Ask,* "What are you angry about in this situation?" *[cr] with "I feel angry that (name what you feel angry about)" (will be on/umb on because client resonates with this disappointment and hurt that his/her needs are not being met).

   d. *Ask,* "What do you really need in your relationship with (name person)?" *[cr] with "I am/have (name the need) in my relationship with (name person)" (will be off/umb off because client doesn't resonate with providing the need or receiving the need).

D. Read or tell the story of remember to bow *p.181*

Ask, "What does this story mean for you?" *[cr] with "I (*name the positive meaning*)" (*will be off/umb off*).

E. Identify the earlier experience being reactivated

Do {a–e} in sequence.

a. *Ask,* "What earlier experience did you have that is similar to the present situation in some way and you were a victim, perpetrator or a fix-it savior?" *[cr] with the earlier experience (*will be on/umb on because client resonates with this experience as though it is still present and as a result the victim, perpetrator, fix-it savior pattern is replicated in the present situation*).

b. *Ask,* "How do you imagine you felt in that earlier experience?" *[cr] with "I continue to feel (*name the feeling*) in the present" (*will be on/umb on because client still resonates with this painful feeling*).

c. *Ask,* "As a result of that earlier painful experience, what negative belief do you imagine you had about (yourself • any perpetrator involved)?" *[cr] (*will be on/umb on because client resonates with this negative belief as being true*).

d. The five inherent needs

(**mcs**) As a result of this earlier experience, (*name client*) stopped resonating with {a–e}:

a. security
b. happiness
c. a sense of achievement
d. love
e. meaning and purpose in life

*[cr] with "I feel (insecure • unhappy • a failure • unloved/unlovable • there is no meaning and purpose in my life)" (*will be on/umb on because client still resonates with the earlier experience when this need(s) was not met*).

e. *Ask*, "In that earlier experience who tried to fix the situation and make things better, but without addressing and resolving the real underlying problem?" *Ask*, "What did the person do to try and fix the situation?" *[**cr**] with "(*Name the person in past who tried to fix the situation*) tries to fix the situation by (*name the fix*), but there is no loving and honest communication, the underlying problem is not addressed or resolved and I continue to try and fix things in the same way" *(will be on/umb on)*.

f. *Ask*, "What do you want instead of that experience?" *Explain:* "Everything is in the mind. That experience is over yet you still carry it around as though it is present. As a result, it is still automatically firing your fight-flight stress response. When you say what you want instead and resonate with it, it creates new neural connections between your limbic brain and your higher brain pre-frontal cortex." *[**cr**] *(will be off/ umb off because client does not resonate with this higher-brain vision of what is possible)*.

F. Read **or** tell the story of the five important words *p.182*
Ask, "What does this story mean for you?" *[**cr**] with "I (*name the positive meaning*)" *(will be off/umb off)*.

G. Identify how client needs to bring the lower brains into sync with the heart and pre-frontal cortex by communicating his/her point of view
Do {a–c} in sequence.
Explain: "When your reptilian and limbic brains are in the service of your heart and the higher pre-frontal cortex brain, every relationship interaction you have with (*name person/others*) will amplify the frequencies of both of you so you experience more closeness, harmony, trust, love and joy. This is made possible when both people honestly and lovingly **communicate** their side of the story and **listen** to each other, free of defensiveness or self-justification, and feel heard and understood."

a. *Ask,* "Communicate your point of view of the upset and any mistake you may have made to (*name person*)."
Practitioner says, "I'm checking you for **communicating** your point of view honestly and lovingly to (*name person*) and being heard." *[**cr**] with "I lovingly communicate my point of view that (*name point of view*) and the mistake I made that (*name mistake*). I feel heard and understood by (*name person*) free of judgments" (*will be off/umb off*).

b. *Ask,* "What is the worst that could happen when you communicate your point of view to (*name person*)?" *[**cr**] (*will be on/umb on for the negative response*).

c. *[**cr**] with "I set appropriate boundaries on (*name person/anyone*) if he/she (punishes me • hurts me • abuses me • coerces me)" (*will be off/umb off*).

H. Identify how client needs to bring his/her lower brains into sync with the heart and pre-frontal cortex brain by understanding the point of view of (*name person*)
Do {a–b} in sequence.
Explain: To activate your pre-frontal cortex you need to move beyond arguments, win-lose, right and wrong and being stuck in your own position. What is important is to give your full attention to listening to (*name person*)'s point of view with understanding, and acknowledge what (*name person*) is feeling and needing.

Each time you do this, your reptilian survival brain and limbic emotional brain are in the service of your higher pre-frontal cortex, which knows that more important than being right is the desire to amplify your frequencies for more love and joy.

Using your pre-frontal cortex and connecting to your heart brings a solution that satisfies both people. But sometimes the resolution to the upset may only be that both of you accept that different people have different perceptions.

This requires that you let go of the upset and make your peace of mind your priority.

a. If the other person is not present, *Ask client,* "What do you imagine (*name person*) wants to communicate with you, and any mistake he/she made?"

Practitioner states, "I'm checking you for **listening** to (*name person*) with empathy and understanding." Tell client, "I am representing (*name person*)."

*[cr] with "(*Name person*) shares his/her point of view that (*name point of view*) and the mistake that (*name the mistake*). I listen with empathy and understanding" *(will be off/umb off because client doesn't resonate with listening to (name person) free of reptilian and limbic brain reactiveness).*

b. *Ask,* "What do you imagine is the worst that could happen when (*name person*) communicates his/her point of view?" *[cr] *(will be on/umb on for the negative response).*

c. *[cr] with "(*Name person*) sets appropriate boundaries on me if I (punish • hurt • abuse • coerce) him/her" *(will be off/umb off).*

I. Identify the resonance with the open-hearted hero, the noble adversary and the wise teacher that is needed
Do {a–c} in sequence.
a. (**mcs**) **The noble adversary way of being is needed?** (versus the perpetrator)
(**mcs**) {1–9}. *[cr] *(will be off/umb off).*
1. I avoid focusing on who is right and who is wrong.
2. I avoid (arguing • becoming reactive).
3. I avoid (labeling • criticizing • blaming) (*name person*).
4. I avoid getting defensive when I don't accept (*name person*)'s perception of what happened.
5. I avoid invalidating (*name person*) and making him/her wrong.

6. I avoid (making excuses for myself • justifying my words and behavior • going into counter-blame and criticism).
7. (I genuinely want to regain a state of harmony with (*name person*) • I am willing to accept that we have two different perceptions and that neither of us is right or wrong).
8. I have to courage to say, 'I want to correct this upset so we can have more connection in our relationship.'
9. I communicate the truth of what I observe in an honest, loving way.

b. (**mcs**) **The open-hearted hero way of being is needed?** (versus the victim)
   (**mcs**) {1–5}. *[**cr**] (*will be off/umb off*).
   1. I communicate my truth to (*name person*) with strength, courage and respect.
   2. (I maintain my calm center and do the right thing • I treat (each person/*name person*) with utmost respect even though he/she has hurt me).
   3. I have the courage to acknowledge that my relationship with (*name person*) is off-track and I communicate that he/she is important to me and that I want us both to come to a new understanding with each other.
   4. I set clear boundaries in a loving and respectful way on negative, judgmental words or behaviors and I encourage mutual communication of our different points of view.
   5. I do not allow myself to be (hurt • abused) in my relationship with (*name person*).

c. (**mcs**) **The wise teacher way of being is needed?** (versus the fix-it savior)
   (**mcs**) {1–11}. *[**cr**] (*will be off/umb off*).
   1. (I avoid projecting what (*name person*) is feeling or needing • I ask (*name person*) what he/she needs).
   2. I listen with patience, and when (*name person*) is complete with communicating their side of the story, I show that I understand their side and also help him/her gain a broader perspective of the situation.

3. (I avoid taking sides • I stay neutral and loving in relation to all those involved in the upset).
4. I teach others by modeling right action.
5. I share my point of view truthfully, lovingly and free of all judgments.
6. I respect myself and all those involved in the problem and I have each person's best interest at heart.
7. I avoid talking negatively about those involved behind their back, unless in a therapeutic way for gaining understanding.
8. I support connection so that those involved in the problem are energized once more by their relationship.
9. I listen more than I talk and then give wise counsel and a new way of understanding the difficult situation.
10. I help (*name person*/others) discover their own best resolution.
11. Before giving any advice, I make sure those involved in the problem want to hear my advice.

J. Identify the Energizing Option needed to bring the frequencies into sync with the coherent triangle
See SPIRAL UP! book for complete list of all Energizing Options.

K. Resonance Repatterning practitioners will now recheck the *[cr] statements and confirm any change in resonance

HOW TO USE THE TRIANGLES OF THE HEART REPATTERNING IN YOUR DAILY LIFE EVEN IF YOU HAVE NOT YET ATTENDED A RESONANCE REPATTERNING SEMINAR

- Whenever you have a relationship problem – small or big – ask yourself whether you are in the victim, perpetrator or fix-it savior role. Observe how you move from one role to another. Read the two stories.

- If you don't have much time, even identifying the perpetrator, victim and fix-it savior resonance involved {*B a b c*} and then doing an Energizing Option to change your resonance, will bring about a shift for you.

- Resonating with the coherent way of being of the open-hearted hero, the noble adversary and the wise teacher {I a b c}is also powerful, and quick to do. Make sure you do an Energizing Option from SPIRAL UP! so you resonate with these empowered ways of being.

- Enjoy seeing people who are difficult for you as a noble adversary – a messenger who brings an important message to you, a message you want to learn from and take to heart. This takes you out of oppositional relationships. You can't change another person. You can only change yourself. Using the Resonance Repatterning tool we move into resonance with our noble adversary, being an opportunity to shift yet another non-coherent pattern that holds us back from being human: fully ourselves – spirit in action.

RR SESSIONS: *If you would like to receive the complete Repatterning with a professional Resonance Repatterning Practitioner, in person or over the phone, go to ResonanceRepatterning.net > Sessions for RR Institute Practitioners worldwide who have listed themselves on the RRI website.*

RR SEMINARS: *If you would like to attend Resonance Repatterning seminars in person or online, so you can use RR effectively on yourself and/or others, go to ResonanceRepatterning.net > Seminars for the list of teachers endorsed by the Resonance Repatterning Institute to teach.*

7. HEART ABUNDANCE

Love is the only integrating power in existence. It is all that can establish order out of chaos or maintain order in chaos.

Starr Daily, *Love Can Open Prison Doors*

As important as business is, family is more important.
As important as success is, peace is more important.
As important as money is, love is more important."

Kristin Zhivago, business coach

Abundance of the heart is totally different from what we usually associate with abundance. It has nothing to do with money, success or attracting what we want.

We will look at five aspects of heart abundance:
1. Abundance as a piece of string
2. Abundance as a state of mind
3. Abundance as giving
4. Abundance as balance of the Five Acupuncture Elements
5. Global abundance as compassion

1. Abundance as a piece of string

There was a group of autistic children who could only stand up with the help of a prop, like a chair. Without the prop they would fall down and wouldn't try to get up again.

Then someone had the idea to tie a rope between the chairs. The experiment was successful. As long as the children held onto the rope, they could walk.

Then a thinner rope was tried with equal success. Finally a piece of string was tied between the chairs, and still the children could walk and move around even though the string was hardly enough to support them.

At this point someone made an imaginative leap and suggested giving each child a small piece of string to hold in their hands.

As long as the autistic children carried a piece of string, they could walk freely.

What these children needed was a feeling of support. When they felt supported they could walk.

If doing the Repatterning, return to {C a} p.

⌒

Rationally, holding a piece string isn't enough support for an autistic child to walk. But our brain is only partially rational.

Most of what we need is not rational at all.

Like Charlie Brown who feels secure as long as he has his blankie, we too have symbols that get us through life – symbols that give us a sense of abundance.

Abundance for the autistic children was having a symbol of support. For almost everything we need and want in life, we too have a symbol of that thing. Some of these symbols work well, and some don't work at all. For instance,

- for many people the symbol of feeling nurtured is food

- a symbol for feeling confident (and as a compensation for low self-worth) may be cocaine or alcohol

- a symbol for comfort or energy to face the day may be cups of coffee

- for the English, a symbol for facing any life challenge is a cup of tea!

- a symbol for love is a bunch of roses

- and for the last two thousand years, the symbol of security for women was a husband – even if he brought no security at all!

Much of our life is about symbols.

What is important is to resonate with symbols that help us – help us walk, feel confident and loved. And we need to transform our resonance with addictive symbols that don't help us. For example, a client used to go to Saks Fifth Avenue once a week and spent $2000. This weekly buying spree symbolized something important for her: a feeling of being valued, up, prosperous, cheerful, important, free. But if she had simply resonated with these positive states, she most likely would not have needed the $2000 symbol for these positive qualities.

It is interesting to look at what we do and ask ourselves what our actions symbolize for us – especially those things we do that don't improve the quality of our life.

2. Abundance as a state of mind

Some years ago there was a documentary on television. They were interviewing an American farmer, asking him what it was like being a farmer in the USA.

The farmer was sitting in his beautiful white-painted farmhouse having dinner with his wife and two children. He was surrounded by hundreds of acres of land.

He said farming was extremely difficult: the cost of insecticides; the cost of the farm equipment; the cost of sending his children to college; and then with droughts and floods you couldn't guarantee your crops. He was filled with worries and very real concerns.

The documentary then cut to a farmer in India. The Indian farmer had a handkerchief-size bit of land, a wife and ten children.

When asked what it was like for him being a farmer in India, he responded with gratitude to God: for his land; for his wonderful wife; for the blessing of his ten children; for earning enough for all of them to eat one meal a day and the joy of selling their fruit and vegetables at the market. He said he had no worries, that everything was God's grace.

If doing the Repatterning, return to {D a} p.212

We know logically that abundance is not about material goods. We know that abundance is a state of mind. But in spite of this, if you ask people what would bring them a feeling of abundance, most people start talking about having more money or having some material goods they need.

In the story of the two farmers, the outcome both farmers want is to provide for their family.

But the farmer in the USA is like the autistic children who cannot stand up and move freely. He doesn't have a positive symbol – the piece of string – that represents the security, faith and self-confidence that would free him from worry.

In spite of this farmer's hundreds of acres, his house and beautiful wife and two children, he is poorer than the Indian farmer who has almost nothing!

On the other hand, the piece of string – the symbol, that represents the Indian farmer's ability to provide for his family – is his gratitude. We could say that his symbol is a positive attitude of contentment and praise: everything is God's will. As a result his state of mind is one of abundant joy and well-being.

What we are seeing here is that the symbol we carry in our heart determines how abundant we feel.

3. Abundance as giving

A powerful story illustrates the third facet of abundance: Giving. Giving our time, our energy, our optimism, the clarity of our thinking, our humor, the power of our listening or our help.

The boss who gave

A friend sent me a newsletter in which she told a story about a boss she once had who perfectly represents this kind of abundance.

She wrote, "One night my boss came to our volunteer Boys and Girls Club board meeting half an hour late, looking a little tired.

"The agenda was full, and there was dissension in the room between the old board members and more visionary younger types. It was not going well for me as CEO, but when my boss arrived, his presence had an amazing effect on everyone.

"He announced that he could only stay a short time as business was calling him away. Then he summarized the most difficult issues and acknowledged everyone's opinion. In the process he cracked a few jokes and used humor to lighten the room.

"We took a vote on the essential items and fifty minutes after he arrived, he excused himself and left. Everyone was in a good mood and sorry to see him leave. However, we were all communicating more effectively, listening to each other and acknowledging each other's point of view.

"Another board member, a senior manager who also worked for my boss, sat at the table dumb-founded. When my boss had left, he said, 'I can't believe what just happened here! That man is about to lose his entire business. He won't know until tomorrow morning if he'll have a cent to his name. I just can't believe he came to this Boys and Girls Club meeting!'

"The next morning I asked my boss how he could have the presence of mind to attend a volunteer meeting when he was facing a potential business disaster.

"He said that his priority of serving the children and his community kept him sane in the cutthroat world of business. He felt that giving in this way had made it possible for him to become a millionaire. He said that keeping his commitment to the kids restored his faith in humanity."

Clearly money was not the source of his abundance.

My friend shared that her boss had a 9th-grade education and his alcoholic father had deserted the family when he was two years old. After building up his business and then almost losing every cent, he later sold it for several million dollars!

If doing the Repatterning, return to {E a} p.212

❧

What was this man's piece of string? The outcome he wanted was to serve – to be of service to children and his community. The feeling he gets from serving is fulfillment.

His symbol, based on this story, is putting children in need first. Serving others is the symbol that nurtures him and that, like the autistic children, lets him walk free in the cutthroat world of big business.

4. **Abundance as balance of our Five Acupuncture Elements**
   As a trained Acupuncturist, I love to use the Five Elements of Chinese Acupuncture – Wood, Fire, Earth, Metal and Water – to find a deeper understanding of how life works.

   Balancing our Five Elements gives us infinite possibilities for abundance.

   Let's look at my friend's boss and imagine the balance of his Five Elements to see what made him abundant from this point of view. And we can use this understanding to become aware of the balance of our own Five Elements so we too can be abundant.

The boss's Wood Element energy
My friend said her boss was always optimistic. No matter what was happening he would say, "Tomorrow is another day."

This strong **Wood** quality of hope and optimism is what he brought to all his interactions at work and in his volunteer service work. People want to be around someone whose energy is naturally harmonized in this optimistic way. He didn't have to try to be optimistic. He simply was optimistic.

The boss's Fire Element energy
He also showed the quality of a balanced **Fire Element:** he was warm and loving and always thought well of people. My friend said he would find a way for everyone to feel part of a group.

He would bring humor to every situation, and even amidst dissension in a board meeting, he would get the group to relax and laugh.

We all have the Fire Element within us. It may need strengthening, but the Fire Element qualities of warmth, humor and connection are there for us as much as they are for this boss.

The boss's Earth Element energy
He also manifested balanced **Earth Element** qualities: serving others, taking care of people, being generous with his time, energy and understanding. Volunteering to be of service to the less fortunate is the hallmark of strong Earth.

Even under the stress of losing his business and not having a cent to his name, he manifested positive Earth qualities: he was relaxed and secure within himself.

My friend also added that if her boss had $1 and you needed it more than he did, he would give it to you. This is the ultimate in Earth energy – when we are recharged by giving and serving.

The boss's Metal Element energy
This man expressed balanced **Metal Element** qualities. My friend said he
had total integrity and lived by his values that the most important thing was
to give something back.

He had been brought up in poverty. The father, who is associated with the
Metal Element, had deserted the family.

He had not received much in terms of schooling or the goods of this world,
yet his values were to give, to serve, to volunteer on boards dedicated
to helping others. And he managed a financially successful business.
All Metal qualities.

The boss's Water Element energy
The night the boss came to the Boys and Girls Club board meeting, when
he didn't know whether his business would survive and if he would have a
cent to his name the next day, he never once mentioned his own troubles.
He didn't even show that he had any personal troubles, besides looking a
little tired.

The **Water Element**, which relates to the Bladder Meridian, is about
containment. This man was able to contain his own troubles so he could give
of himself to others.

The Water Element is also about listening. My friend's boss was a man who
listened to each person's opinion with respect (Metal) and helped everyone
reach an amicable resolution.

For myself, when I hear about people like this, I say to myself, 'Well, he must be
special. I couldn't be like that' and I start seeing all my Five Element deficiencies!

But the fact is we all have the same Meridian and Five Element energies within us.

When these frequencies are out of sync, the weakened qualities of the Elements and Meridians will naturally show up. But when the frequencies of our Elements and Meridians are balanced, the coherent qualities of the Elements and Meridians express themselves automatically.

When we resonate with these qualities and put them into practice, we begin to live our true nature.

5. Global abundance as compassion

Global abundance is about compassion for others' suffering and doing whatever we can to alleviate suffering.

The seventeenth-century poet John Donne wrote, "No man is an island unto himself."

If we want global abundance, we need to recognize that we are all one. As modern day physicists have discovered, there is no separation. We are all energetically connected. Therefore every positive or negative thought is a frequency that affects others. Every positive action, no matter how small, is significant in creating life-enhancing change.

David Lloyd George said, "Anything can be achieved in small, deliberate steps. But there are times you need the courage to take a great leap. You can't cross a chasm in two small jumps."

If we truly want global abundance, we will need the courage to take a great leap. This leap is about me: what can I do within myself, in my life, in how I relate, in what I eat, in the kinds of thoughts I project that will have a positive impact for humanity (which includes animals, plants and the earth).

More and more people are finally beginning to face the fact that we are at one of the great crossroads in our global history. Al Gore's film, *An Inconvenient Truth*, helped get our attention.

Scientific facts that impact our health and global abundance

We need to be aware of eleven scientific facts:

1. There are now ten times more food animals than people in the world – 60 billion cows, pigs, chickens, turkeys, sheep, etc. 60,000,000,000 of them being raised and killed to provide people with meat, eggs and milk.

2. Food animals need a lot of land, both for grazing and for crops to feed them with. This means clearing vast acreages of forested areas.

3. 70% of the Amazon rainforest clearing is for the animal grazing industry, not to mention the clearing of forested lands all across the USA and most other countries in Europe, Africa, South America and Asia. Much of this activity, especially the Amazon rainforest clearing, is to provide meat for the US market.

4. When forests are cleared on the present large scale, it radically disturbs the health of soil, water and air: deforestation and overgrazing result in erosion, which results in a loss of topsoil and the fertility of the soil and mineral deficiencies in the plants that live from the soil's nutrients.

   Clearing forests also leads to a lessening of rainfall (trees attract rain); to a lowering of the water table; to heating up of exposed soil, which results in a loss of soil fertility. In addition, clearing forests leads to the disappearance of year-round streams, lakes and rivers, and the decline or decimation of multiple plant systems and animal species.

5. 60 billion food animals (injected or fed with growth hormones, fattening agents, antibiotics and a total of four hundred and fifty different drugs) produce huge quantities of fecal matter and urine, which seriously contaminate rivers, groundwater, wells, reservoirs, lakes and oceans.

   Animal fecal matter and urine generate 37% of all human-induced methane – the impact of this is 23 times worse than carbon dioxide. Fecal matter and urine produce 65% of the world's nitrous oxide, which has 296 times the global warming potential of carbon dioxide. Nitrous oxide produces 64% of all ammonia emissions, which causes acid rain that destroys vast ecosystems.

6. The animal food industry generates 18% of the world's total carbon dioxide – almost half as much again as all forms of transportation pollution combined. The animal food industry is a leading contributor to global warming, greenhouse gas emissions and carbon dioxide pollution – again, **even more detrimental than the entire transportation industry combined.**

7. Animals being raised for food consume a lot of water. A vegan – someone who does not eat any animal products – could run their shower all day and all night, every day of the week for a year, and they would still consume less water than someone whose diet is based on meat and dairy products!

8. People in the USA consume the most meat and animal products in the world (including meat, fish, eggs, milk and milk products) and the USA is also high on the list of countries with the largest numbers of people suffering from chronic diseases like heart disease, cancer, diabetes, arthritis and osteoporosis.

9. During WW II when meat was difficult to obtain, the death rate in countries like Holland and Belgium was lower than its pre-war level, in spite of war-related deaths and a general shortage of food.

   After the war when meat became available again, the death rate quickly returned to its higher pre-war level! The two main variables here are that during the war people were eating less food and were eating little or no animal products.

10. Multiple health studies round the world during the last seven decades, printed in highly respected medical journals in the USA, Britain, Canada and elsewhere, have shown conclusively that people – of all ages and all occupations (including children, the elderly, and world-class athletes and triathlon winners) – are far more healthy on an exclusively plant-based diet of vegetables, fruit, seeds, nuts and grains like quinoa, millet and buckwheat, than people anywhere in the world who eat meat, fish, eggs and milk products.

11. The China Study – the largest research project ever accomplished, conducted jointly by Cornell University, Oxford University and the Chinese Academy of Preventive Medicine over a twenty-year period, proved that an animal-based diet is associated with disease. They found that the lower the percentage of animal-based foods, the greater the health of the individuals.

    One of the authors of the China Study, T. Colin Campbell, states, "There are powerful, influential and enormously wealthy industries that stand to lose a vast amount of money if Americans start shifting to a plant-based diet."

We must remember, we are temporary visitors on this earth. Global awareness is about being conscious of our impact on 'the seven generations' to come. This kind of heightened awareness is what Dr. Albert Schweitzer called "reverence for life."

Albert Einstein said, "Nothing will benefit human health and increase the chances for survival of life on earth as much as the evolution to a vegetarian diet."

Spiritual teachers have said, "How can we have peace of mind when we cause suffering and pain to animals" through our desire to eat them?

Now, at this historic juncture, if we as a species want to continue living on this planet, we must think seriously about what we eat and the repercussions our choices have on all life forms, our planet and our health.

For those who are ready to jump the chasm towards global abundance, as David Lloyd George advised, and reduce or eliminate their animal-based diet, we need to be well-informed.

$\backsim$

FURTHER READING AND INFORMATION

Victoria Boutenko. *Green for Life*. Fascinating research, readable and practical. You don't have to change your regular diet. Just start drinking blended fruit and raw organic vegetables (she gives you easy one-minute recipes) and quite naturally you will find your craving for meat, fish, eggs and milk diminishing.

Also by Victoria, Igor, Sergei and Valya Boutenko. *Raw Family, A True Story of Awakening*. An interesting story of their family's move from sickness to health.

Colin Campbell. *The China Study*. I've heard that people, including many doctors, who read this study immediately become vegetarian. Be warned!

Starr Daily. *Love Can Open Prison Doors*.

Rebecca Hammons. *Being Vegetarian* (Radha Soami Satsang Beas, 2017).

John Robbins. *Diet for a New America*.

Richard Schulze. *Creating Powerful Health Naturally* (2008, HerbDoc.com).

Christopher Vasey, N.D. *The Acid-Alkaline Diet for Optimum Health: Restore Your Health by Creating pH Balance in your Diet*.

Dr. N.W. Walker. *Become Younger* (Dr. Walker died at 106 years of age!). Norwalk Press, Prescott, Arizona. 1949.

Check out the **Physicians Committee for Responsible Medicine** at www.pcrm.org for up-to-date vegetarian and vegan nutritional information from vegan medical doctors on a range of health conditions (including cancer, heart disease, high blood pressure, over-weight and diabetes), as well as dozens of tasty low-fat recipes and other practical support to help you transition to a healthy non-animal diet. **Physicians Committee for Responsible Medicine** is doing heroic work getting healthy vegetarian and vegan foods served in schools and successfully getting animal experiments abolished in medical schools throughout the US and military. An inspired group of conscious doctors!

UN Food and Agriculture Organization report, "Livestock's Long Shadow: Environmental Issues and Options" (available online)

Video: Forks Over Knives (Netflix.com)

Video: What the Health (youtube.com)

Film: One Man, One Cow, One Planet

7. HEART ABUNDANCE REPATTERNING

A. Name the abundance outcome you want
Do {a–b} in sequence.
a. *Ask,* "What do you want for yourself in your life – an outcome you want
that would make you feel truly abundant?"
*[**cr**] with "I (*name the outcome wanted*) and I feel truly abundant"
*(will be off/ umb off because client doesn't resonate with having heart
abundance).*

b. *Ask,* "How would doing/having (*name {A a}*) make you feel?"
*[**cr**] *(will be off/umb off).*

B. Name your problem
Do {a–b} in sequence.
a. *Ask,* "What is the problem you are facing in your life regarding
abundance or lack of abundance?"
[**cr**] *(will be on/umb on because client resonates with a lack of abundance).*

b. *Ask,* "What negative action do you do, or what negative habit or attitude
do you have that you have not been able to overcome at this time?"
*[**cr**] with "I choose (*name the negative action, habit or attitude*) over
having the heart abundance of (*name the positive outcome wanted in
{A a}*)" *(will be on/umb on).*

C. Read or tell the story of Abundance as a piece of string *p.197*
Do {a–b} in sequence.
a. *Ask,* "What did you learn from this story in terms of abundance in your
life?" *[**cr**] with "I (*name the learning*)" *(will be off/umb off).*

b. **The core need and the symbol**
Explain: The core need of the autistic children was to feel supported.

Holding a piece of string was a symbol that represented support, and
which therefore allowed them to achieve the outcome of walking.

We all need to resonate with our own core need and the positive symbol of what we need. This changes our actions as it did with the children.

Ask, "What is your core need?" *[**cr**] with "I (*name the core need*)" *(will be off/umb off)*.

Ask, "What symbol represents (*name the core need*)?" *[**cr**] with "(I visualize/hold onto/take in (*name the symbol*), which allows me to (*name the need*) and (*name the outcome {A a}*)" *(will be off/umb off)*.

D. Identify Abundance as a state of mind that is needed
Do {a–c} in sequence.
a. Read Abundance as a state of mind *p.199*
    Ask, "In what way are you not fully enjoying the abundance that you have?" *[**cr**] *(will be on/umb on)*.

b. *Ask,* "What actions are you doing that undermine enjoying the abundance you have?" *[**cr**] *(will be on/umb on)*.

c. *Ask,* "What positive attitude would allow you to feel abundant no matter what difficulties you face?" *[**cr**] with "I (*name the positive attitude*)" *(will be off/umb off)*.

E. Identify Abundance as giving that is needed
Do {a–c} in sequence.
a. Read or tell the story of Abundance as giving *p.201*
    Ask, "What did you learn from this story?" *[**cr**] with "I (*name the learning but omit 'learn'*)" *(will be off/umb off)*.

    Ask, "What can you give when facing (*name the present problem {B a}*) that would make a positive difference for you and (*name person*)?" *[**cr**] with "When (*name the problem {B a}*), I (*name what client gives*)" *(will be off/umb off)*.

b. Read the story of Greg Mortenson and Abundance as giving *p.213*

Greg Mortenson, author of *Three Cups of Tea* and *Stones into Schools,* describes his often harrowing journeys in remote mountain areas of Pakistan and Afghanistan. Over the years he created relationships with the Muslim elders and villagers, convincing them of the importance of educating their girl children – who had never received an education before this point.

Greg's vision was that one girl from a distant village, the first literate girl in her community, would open the way for hundreds of other girls to follow. As he says, "You educate one girl and you change the world."

In 1994, trying to raise funds for the first school, he gave a talk in a US elementary school where his mother was the principal. The next day a fourth-grader brought his piggy bank to school and emptied out all the pennies, donating them to Greg to help build the school in Pakistan. The other children caught the spirit of giving and Pennies4Peace was born.

Now, as the co-founder of Central Asia Institute, Greg and the CAI have at this time built 200 schools. One of the girls from the remote Wakhan Corridor in Afghanistan recently arrived in the US to begin a Master's level Fulbright scholarship.

The power of grassroots, Greg says, is that a person says "**I can do this one act,**" instead of feeling overwhelmed by "**What can I possibly do?**" He says we all have the power to set an intention for positive change – to make a difference. In this way, he says, people create hope and the potential for one more person to rise.

⌒

Even though the situation in Pakistan, Afghanistan and Tajikistan appears dire, the Central Asia Institute brings hope that:
• no crisis is insoluble

- no amount of assistance is too small

- no act of kindness is without its reward

For example in Lokhai, Afghanistan, there are 1,000 children. There are only a few elders in the village as the rest of the men died in the fighting. Water and food are scarce. At the end of a dirt road, located on a barren plateau, is the Lokhai primary school. It has no school building and only two teachers. But hundreds of children sit on cotton rugs on the bare ground in the hot sun, focused on their teacher. Hope for these people lies in the next generation.

An American child in Ritchie Park School (that donated their pennies and raised $2,360.59 to help the CAI children go to school) said, "Everyone needs to learn humanity. I mean, one single penny can change someone's life." A teacher at Ritchie Park School commented that "After all the pennies had been collected and sent to Central Asia Institute, I would hear students talking about big ideas like kindness and how they had an impact on another child's life.... Our job as educators isn't to tell children what to think, it's to empower them to think for themselves.... Then they are on their way to be the best they can be, and they help others in the process."

Abundance through the balance of our Five Elements involves this kind of empathy, generosity, kindness, learning, empowerment, hope, vision – and above all, networks of human beings who want to connect and express their love in action.

c. *Ask,* "What did you learn from this story?" *[**cr**] with "I (*name the positive learning but omit 'learn'*)" (*will be off/umb off*).

F. Identify Abundance as the balance of the Five Elements
(**mcs**) {a–e} for the Element(s) needed.
a. Wood Element (**mcs**) {1–6}.
  1. I am always hopeful and optimistic no matter what.

2. I am a change maker.
3. (I choose life • I support what is life-giving).
4. I go into action and do my best to reach my goal, no matter what.
5. I move into new beginnings with a sense of excitement.
6. (I take the space I need to grow into my potential • I let go of seeing myself as insignificant • I see each positive action I do as making a positive difference).

b. **Fire Element** (**mcs**) {1–11}.
   1. I help others relax and laugh.
   2. I laugh in the face of my fears.
   3. I am warm and loving with everyone.
   4. I help everyone to feel a part of the group.
   5. I stay connected to my heart's compassion for myself and others.
   6. I feel safe and protected and I help others feel safe.
   7. I sort out what is rich for my heart and what isn't.
   8. In challenging situations I communicate with a sense of ease and pleasure.
   9. I am energized (being with people • being a loving presence for others).
   10. I create networks for positive change.
   11. I listen to each person's point of view with understanding.

c. **Earth Element** (**mcs**) {1–6}.
   1. I help others.
   2. I support others in their time of need.
   3. I trust that I am looked after and that my basic needs are met.
   4. I relax.
   5. I am generous, appropriately giving of my time, energy and resources to those in need.
   6. I am of service.

d. **Metal Element** (**mcs**) {1–7}.
   1. I do right action.
   2. I put right action before my need to win and be the best.

3. I maintain my integrity in all circumstances.
4. I follow my truth and live my truth in action.
5. I respect each person I meet • I am worthwhile • I respect myself).
6. I live with reverence for all life forms on earth.
7. I am honest and direct in my dealings with others.

e. **Water Element** (**mcs**) {1–8}.
   1. I have the courage to persevere round every obstacle.
   2. I am calm in crisis situations.
   3. I have the courage to do whatever I can do for our global village.
   4. I have the clarity of mind to see beyond the present fearful situation.
   5. I have the courage to use my power, energy and drive to keep moving forward.
   6. I have the power to act on what is right.
   7. I listen carefully and bring clarity.
   8. I contain (my own troubles • my reactiveness in a challenging situation) in order to create a forward movement for the person concerned or the group.

G. Identify Heart Abundance as global compassion

Explain: It is important to understand that compassion involves a reverence for life and an awareness of the suffering of all beings – human, animal and in nature. Compassion is not about guilt or feeling judged. It is about opening our heart to whatever positive action we want and are ready to do at this moment – no matter how small – that reflects our own personal reverence for life.

(**mcs**) {a–k} for the awareness of suffering that is needed.

a. **#1: General awareness**
   Worldwide there are sixty billion cows, pigs, chickens, turkeys and sheep, which are raised and killed for people who eat meat, eggs and milk products.

b. **#2: Awareness of suffering in dairy factories**
   Dairy factories are not farms.

- Cows are kept indoors all year round. They become lame, develop mastitis and these normally peaceful animals become aggressive.

- Cows naturally live 20–25 years. Dairy cows confined to milking stations, subjected to constant artificial insemination and pregnancies, are worn out in 4–5 years, at which point they are made into low-grade meat products.

- Calves are separated from their mothers a few hours after birth. Those not needed for milk production are confined in small veal cages two feet wide, with their heads chained. The calves cannot walk, turn around or lie down comfortably. Their muscles don't develop, which keeps their meat tender – the delicacy demanded by veal eaters. They are fed synthetic formula to keep their meat pale and anemic.

c. **#3: Awareness of suffering for chickens, ducks and turkeys**
   - Tens of thousands of birds are crammed together in a tiny space in which they are scarcely able to move.

   - The sheds reek of ammonia from bird droppings, which burn the lungs and eyes and cause blindness. (The workers have to wear gas masks.)

   - Under stress, the birds feather peck. To prevent this their beaks, which are filled with nerve endings, are sheared off with a hot blade.

   - Egg-laying birds spend their life in metal battery cages in artificial lighting – to extend the hours of 'daylight' in order to increase egg production.

   - When egg production declines, the birds are slaughtered.

   - Female hens are genetically manipulated to create large breasts and thighs for meat-eating purposes.

   - So-called "free range" means the birds have access to a small area of outdoor space. But with tens of thousands of hens in a shed and one small outside plot, the birds are not ranging freely as we visualize it.

- Male chicks in the egg production industry can't lay eggs so they are put through meat grinders while still alive, or gassed, or suffocated in trash cans. Birds destined for human food are shackled upside-down on a conveyor belt leading to an electrified water bath, meant to stun the birds before they reach the mechanical neck cutter. The US Dept. of Agriculture states that "millions miss the blades and drown in tanks of scalding water while still conscious."

- Fifty billion chickens are slaughtered for human consumption worldwide.

- Two hundred and thirty-nine million are slaughtered for human consumption in the USA alone.

d. **#4: Awareness of suffering for fish**
- With current fishing practices, 230,000 marine life species have already been destroyed. Scientists estimate that unless these practices change, we will have fishless oceans by 2048.

- With industrial fishing, a single vessel hauls in 50 tons of ocean animals in a few minutes.

- Beam trawling involves large weighted nets, 40 feet high (approximately 13 meters), which are dragged across the seabed 6,000 feet below the surface. The nets crush everything in their path for the sake of the few profitable fish on demand.

- The change in water pressure as the nets are raised can push stomachs and intestines out of the mouths and anuses of the fish and push their eyes out of their sockets.

- On deck the killing continues: cutting off heads, electrical stunning, with the fish not intended for sale being thrown back into the sea – mangled, dying or dead. **This "by-catch" is the majority of the fish caught.**

- If a plate were to hold all the fish killed for one roll of tuna sushi, it would need to be 5 feet (almost 2 meters) long.

e. **#5: Awareness of suffering in fish farms**
  • Special types of fish are cultivated in pens, without the problem of the by-catch.

  • However, the fish are crammed into a small space where they can only swim in the equivalent area of a bath tub, instead of the hundreds and even thousands of miles they normally swim every year.

  • Over-crowding results in about one-third of the fish dying of disease.

  • Fish feces and sea lice cause infection.

  • The fish are fed antibiotics, causing antibiotic resistance in humans – a serious medical problem.

  • Sea lions and seals, attracted to the pens, are exterminated.

  • Porpoises and dolphins get caught in the nets surrounding the pens and are exterminated.

f. **#6: Awareness of suffering caused by methane poisoning – manure overwhelm**
  • A 200 pound pig (approximately 90 kilos) creates about 14 pounds (6 kilos) of feces per day.

  • An average hog farm has 80,000 pigs. This means that 1,120,000 pounds of feces is produced each day on one hog farm.

  • The feces and urine are collected in lagoons where they emit toxic gases like ammonia and methane. The fecal waste – along with the antibiotics fed to the pigs, plus dangerous microbes, nitrate pollution and drug-resistant bacteria – is sprayed on nearby farmland. As the land cannot absorb and break down the excess toxic waste, it runs off into lakes and streams, where it poisons or kills fish and poisons groundwater.

  • The Food and Agriculture Organization of the United Nations states "Pollution of soil and water with pathogens and heavy metals is generally caused by poor manure management."

- Cows produce 250–500 liters (66–132 gallons) of methane per cow per day. There are now about 1.5 billion cows in the world. One dairy farm in the USA with 2,500 cows produces about the same amount of waste as a city of 411,000 people. But human waste is treated before being returned to the water system. Animal waste is either untreated or minimally treated.

- In summary: 60 billion food animals (injected or fed with growth hormones, fattening agents, antibiotics, and a total of 450 different drugs in addition to GMO feed) produce astronomical amounts of fecal matter and urine, which seriously impact the air and groundwater, rivers, reservoirs, lakes and oceans with methane, killing fish and causing disease in humans.

g. **#7: Awareness of suffering caused by over-consumption of water**
- Clean water is becoming scarce: we are using more water than can be replaced by natural cycles.

- Raising animals for food accounts for 27–33% of all fresh water consumption in the world.

- Almost one-third of all fresh water in the world is used for irrigating crops grown solely to feed animals.

- More water is used to grow alfalfa and hay for animal feed than is required for all the vegetable and fruit production in the USA.

- It has been estimated that it takes 1,000 gallons of water to produce 1 gallon of milk; 2,500 gallons of water to produce 1 lb of beef. In contrast, it takes 25 gallons to produce 1 lb of wheat for human consumption.

- With 60 billion animals raised for human consumption, it is clear that this way of living is not sustainable.

h. #8: Awareness of suffering caused by forest clearing

- The world's rainforests have been called the lungs of the world, maintaining the balance of oxygen and carbon dioxide needed for life to exist.

- Because trees attract rain, clearing forests (at the present rate of more than 1 acre per second) leads to less rainfall. Lack of rain lowers the water table, heats up the exposed soil and leads to the disappearance of year-round streams, lakes and rivers. Viktor Schauberger, who studied the impact on streams of removing trees, predicted in the 1930s that one day people would pay several dollars for a bottle of water. Scientists laughed at his predictions.

- About three-quarters of the rainfall in tropical forests returns to the atmosphere through the cycle of evaporation. After deforestation, the land returns only one-quarter of the rainfall. The denuded earth cannot absorb rainfall, which leads to floods, with excess water and topsoil ending up in the oceans, rather than replenishing the underground aquifers we depend on for life.

- Ninety-one percent of rainforest destruction is for animal grazing and feedcrops for animals – 8 feet of forest is cleared for one-quarter pound of hamburger meat!

- Once forests are cleared, the denuded land yields animal feedcrops for 1–4 years, after which time the soil becomes barren.

i. #9: Awareness of suffering caused by climate change and greenhouse gases

- The sun bombards the earth with radiation and heat.

- Some of this heat is reflected back into space.

- Some of this reflected heat is trapped by land, oceans, water vapor, methane, ozone, carbon dioxide and nitrogen oxide.

- Without this heat retention, the average surface temperature of the earth would be –6 degrees centigrade (21 degrees Fahrenheit), not the normal 15 degrees centigrade (59 degrees Fahrenheit). In other words, too cold to support plant growth.

- In the last 100 years, heat-trapping gases have increased exponentially, causing the atmosphere to heat up (i.e., global warming). These heat-containing gases no longer allow for the balanced escape of heat.

- Thirteen percent of all greenhouse gases comes from transportation. Eighteen percent of all greenhouse gases comes from the livestock industry – more than all the planes, trains, trucks and cars in the world.

- Animal fecal matter and urine generates 37% of methane gas, the impact of which is twenty-three times worse than carbon dioxide, which was previously thought to be the most toxic.

- Animal fecal matter and urine produces 65% of the world's nitrous oxide, which has 296 times the global warming potential of carbon dioxide.

- Nitrous oxide produces 64% of all ammonia emissions, which causes acid rain that destroys vast ecosystems. Nitrous oxide remains in the atmosphere for 150 years.

j. **#10: Awareness of physical needs for protein, B12, iron and energy**
- Unless starving, it is difficult to be deficient in **protein**, which is found in every food: nuts, seeds, vegetables, grains, fruit and even baked potatoes. One forgets that the largest animals in the world are vegetarian. Where do elephants and rhinos get their protein?
  - There are numerous vegetarian protein-rich foods, such as tempeh, tofu, humus, quinoa, amaranth, millet, pumpkin seeds, sunflower seeds, hemp seeds, sesame seeds, nuts, peas and beans, artichokes, asparagus, spinach.

  - Most people eat an excess of protein. Renowned researcher T. Colin Campbell could turn cancer on and off simply by increasing and decreasing protein intake in test animals.

- **Vitamin B12** is essential for nerves, the brain, DNA synthesis and for healthy red blood cells. B12 is produced by microorganisms in human and animal small intestines and is also found in healthy organic soil and unpolluted streams.
  - Animals, which no longer drink from unpolluted streams or graze on grass, are deficient in B12. In addition, B12 in meat is mostly destroyed by cooking.
  - Pesticides kill available B12 in nature.
  - Antibiotics destroy B12 in the gut in both meat-eaters and vegans.
  - We don't need much B12 – and if tested to be deficient, a B12 supplement is called for or a life-style change so the gut flora in the intestines are able to produce B12 naturally.

- **Iron** is needed by our brain and nervous system.
  - Researcher Dr. Reed Mangels states that "vegetarians do not have a higher incidence of iron deficiency than do meat eaters."
  - Meat contains heme iron. Plants contain non-heme iron, which is easily absorbed with no danger of excess or toxic reactions.
  - The American Association of Cancer Research states that "heme iron, present in meat, promotes colorectal cancer." Heme iron causes potentially toxic reactions in the colon.
  - Plant-based foods high in non-heme iron are: tofu, spinach, green leafy vegetables (kale, chard, etc.), dried peas, beans and broccoli.

- **Energy:** More and more athletes at the peak of their athletic performance are becoming vegan because it gives them more energy, a quicker recovery time and the ability to train harder. People like Scott Jurek (the world's leading ultra marathon runner), Billie Jean King (winner of 39 Grand Slam titles), Martina Navratilova (world's number one ranking women's tennis player, holding that position longer than any other player), worldclass body builders, swimmers, cyclists and football players are vegans – none is deficient in protein, B12, iron or energy!

k. #10: Hope and compassion are options
- Vegetarian, Paul McCartney, said "If slaughterhouses had glass walls, everyone would be vegetarian."

- We must face the fact that we are enabling an animal holocaust, the likes of which has never been seen on our planet before.

- Our taste for meat and fish is destroying forests, waterways, oceans, the air we breathe, our health and animal life.

- Climate change is already causing devastation – and will cause more devastation in the future if we do nothing.

- We can no longer say "I didn't know." Denial is not an option. Compassion, hope and positive action by each of us, in whatever way we can manage, **is** an option.

H. Identify the Heart Abundance action that client is ready to take

Do {a–b} in sequence.

a. *Explain:* If you cut a holographic film of, let's say an apple, into four pieces and shine a light through each piece, you will see the original whole apple. Unlike a photo that can be cut into pieces, you can never divide the image of a holographic apple, no matter how many times you cut the film into pieces.

We too are a hologram, created from frequencies of light. And like a hologram we too are indivisible – whether human, animal, plant or one of millions of minuscule soil organisms that maintain the balance of nature. We are all one.

Like a hologram, if we change one part, we change the whole.

A spiritual adept said: if we changed our thinking to the positive, this would change the world.

When we change our thinking, it changes our actions. And however insignificant our individual positive action may seem, on an energy level every action has an immediate effect – on our self, our community, our country and the global village of all life forms on this earth.

Quantum change is always tiny, but because we are what new physics calls a 'non-linear system', it only takes a small input of energy at the right time and place to have a huge system wide effect (called the Butterfly Effect).

Quantum change is an unexpected leap from one state to another, with no transition in between. So we cannot predict the outcome of our positive thoughts and actions on global abundance!

b. Remember what Greg Mortenson said: Instead of saying, "What can I do" say, **"I can do this one act."** And the powerful words of former Prime Minister David Lloyd George: "Anything can be achieved in small deliberate steps. **But there are times when you need the courage to take a great leap. You can't cross a chasm in two small steps."**

Ask, "Is there any compassionate action you feel ready to take that will have a positive effect in terms of the well-being of all forms of life – whether human, animal, plant or soil?" *[**cr**] *(will be off/umb off)*.

I. Identify the fears that stop client from manifesting heart abundance
Do {a–b} in sequence.
a. Ask, "What are you afraid of if you went into action for one or more of the ten facts {H a–k}?" *[**cr**] *(will be on/umb on)*.

b. (**mcs**) {1–5} for the Bach Flower non-coherence involved and the coherence needed.
    1. **Aspen fear: fear and anxiety of an unknown origin**
       a. (**mcs**) **A non-coherent Aspen fear is blocking client's heart abundance?** (**mcs**) {1–6}.

1. I am suddenly afraid for no specific reason.
2. I am nervous and anxious.
3. I wake up in fear or terror from a bad dream, sometimes trembling and sweating.
4. I am afraid of death and disaster.
5. I am hypersensitive and over-imaginative and can go into a paralyzing terror.
6. I am afraid of confiding in others about my fears because there is no reason for them.

b. (mcs) Coherent Aspen courage is needed in order to create a new sense of true abundance? (mcs) {1–4}.
   1. I have an inner confidence.
   2. I enjoy adventure and new experiences.
   3. I experience the joy of life, the joy of death and the joy of love.
   4. I can move through any danger and difficulty unafraid because I am supported by love.

2. Mimulus fear: fear of known things
   a. (mcs) A non-coherent Mimulus fear is blocking client's heart abundance? (mcs) {1–4}.
      1. I am afraid of (illness • death • accidents • the dark • growing old • other – *ask:* What is the known thing you are afraid of?).
      2. I am shy and retiring and become tongue-tied around people.
      3. I tend to (blush • laugh nervously about (*name what embarrasses client*) • feel embarrassed by (*name what embarrasses*).
      4. I hide my fears.

   b. (mcs) Coherent Mimulus courage is needed in order to create a new sense of abundance? (mcs) {1–4}.
      1. I have a quiet courage that allows me to face (my trials • others' reactions to me) with humor and confidence.

2. I stand up for myself and what I believe in.
3. I enjoy my life free of fear, once my emotions are under my control.
4. I know (when to withdraw • when I need to be alone).

3. **Red Chestnut fear: fear for others**
   a. (**mcs**) **A non-coherent Red Chestnut fear is blocking client's heart abundance?** (**mcs**) {1–5}.
      1. I fear the worst for my loved ones.
      2. I turn a minor complaint into a major problem.
      3. I worry about other people's problems.
      4. Because of my fears, I tend to force my (help • solutions) onto others.
      5. (If someone is late I fear the worst • If someone goes on holiday, I am afraid something bad will happen to them).

   b. (**mcs**) **Coherent Red Chestnut courage is needed in order to create a new sense of abundance?** (**mcs**){1–4}.
      1. I care for my loved ones with compassion and positive thoughts.
      2. I radiate positive thoughts and health to all.
      3. I am calm even in an emergency.
      4. I give help when asked.

4. **Cherry Plum fear: fear of the mind giving way and breaking down**
   a. (**mcs**) **A non-coherent Cherry Plum fear is blocking client's heart abundance?** (**mcs**){1–6}.
      1. I feel depressed.
      2. I am in despair.
      3. I am afraid of losing my sanity.
      4. I am highly strung and afraid I could hurt myself or someone else.
      5. I am afraid of my violent impulses and being abusive.
      6. I explode in sudden outbursts of rage.

b. (**mcs**) **Coherent Cherry Plum courage is needed in order to create a new sense of abundance?** (**mcs**){1–4}.
   1. I have a calm, quiet inner strength.
   2. I maintain my sanity through extreme conditions.
   3. I come to terms with my inner conflicts.
   4. I am receptive to inner guidance.

5. **Rock Rose fear: terror**
   a. (**mcs**) **A non-coherent Rock Rose fear is blocking client's heart abundance?** (**mcs**){1–4}.
      1. I am frozen with fear after (a natural disaster • sudden illness • a mugging • an accident • witnessing an accident • abuse).
      2. I feel helpless and terrified in the face of (a natural disaster • a sudden illness • a mugging • an accident • witnessing an accident • abuse).
      3. (I have night terrors • I experience sheer terror).
      4. I become exhausted from long-term terror.

   b. (**mcs**) **Coherent Rock Rose courage is needed in order to create a new sense of abundance?** (**mcs**){1–4}.
      1. I have great courage and presence of mind.
      2. I am willing to risk my life to help others.
      3. I have a strong will and character.
      4. In an emergency I am calm and give myself fully to aid others in their time of great need.

J. Identify the birth note Energizing Option needed to create new and positive neural pathways for Heart Abundance
Do {a–d} in sequence.
   a. (**mcs**) **Client needs to understand the importance of toning his/her birth note to reconnect to the heart?**
   Explain: Toning notes has a positive effect on the mind and feelings as well as the physical body. Dr. Alfred Tomatis discovered that high-frequency vocal sounds recharge the brain through direct bone conduction as well as externally through the ears.
   See ResonanceRepatterning.net e-Store for the chromatic toner.

b. Information needed for toning the birth note

- Ask client for their date of birth and find client's four birth notes on the Birth Note Chart: the note that corresponds with the birth month, the note that is opposite the birth note (known as the reciprocal) and the two notes on either side of the reciprocal note (known as reciprocal by light).
  If you know how to muscle check, you can (**mcs**) which of these four notes you need to tone. If not, intuitively choose one of these four notes.

- (**mcs**) for the color(s) needed for the CYW Lenses – often a color relating to one or more of the birth notes.

- (**mcs**) for the vowel sound needed (oo • or • ah • eh • ee • or humming). Make the sound nasal.

- (**mcs**) for the chakra center where you need to feel the sound vibrating: (Base of the Spine • Pelvic • Solar Plexus • Heart • Throat • Brow • Crown) chakra.

c. How To:

- Client puts on CYW Lenses

- Clients does the chest opening movement: arms extended in front of chest, palms facing. Draw the elbows back and slightly down, in a vigorous movement. Repeat five times.

- Client sits and with thumbs touches the Heart Meridian acupuncture point, Utmost Source, at the armpit behind the tendon.

- Client tones his/her birth note.

- Instead of toning the birth note, RR practitioners may (**mcs**) to use a Tuning Fork for the birth note: heard (and over which ear), held over a particular Chakra energy center, a vertebra, an Acupuncture Mu point or other Acupuncture Element point.

BIRTH NOTE CHART

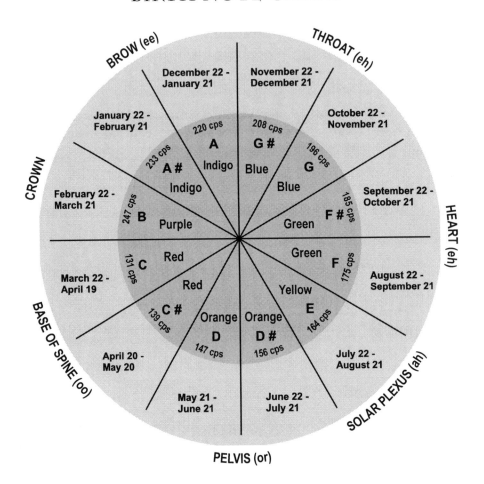

HOW TO USE THE HEART ABUNDANCE REPATTERNING IN YOUR DAILY LIFE
EVEN IF YOU HAVE NOT YET ATTENDED A RESONANCE REPATTERNING SEMINAR

- Be aware of your core need and the positive symbol that represents that need.

- Be aware of the positive mental attitude that brings you a sense of abundance – and make sure you resonate with it.

- Ask yourself, "What can I give today? Who can I give support / time / inspiration / loving thoughts to?"

- When you have an abundance issue, go to the section on the Five Elements and bring them back into balance.

- Every time you go into fear, check the Bach Flower essences for the type of fear involved. Take the remedy or change your resonance with an Energizing Option.

- Do yourself a favor and watch *What the Health* on YouTube. It may save your health or the health of someone you know.

- Begin to practice abundance for the whole planet in your own way: water awareness; solar substitutes; as much as possible limiting the use of electricity; eating more plant-based foods; eating less meat, fish and dairy; exploring new possibilities for natural organic farming methods and reforestation, etc.

RR SESSIONS: *If you would like to receive the complete Repatterning with a professional Resonance Repatterning Practitioner, in person or over the phone, go to ResonanceRepatterning.net > Sessions for RR Institute Practitioners worldwide who have listed themselves on the RRI website.*

RR SEMINARS: *If you would like to attend Resonance Repatterning seminars in person or online, so you can use RR effectively on yourself and/or others, go to ResonanceRepatterning.net > Seminars for the list of teachers endorsed by the Resonance Repatterning Institute to teach.*

8. THE JOY-FILLED HEART

His place in her arms is the expected place, known to his inmost sense as *his* place, and what he experiences while he is in arms is acceptable to his continuum, fulfills his current needs, and contributes correctly to his development....When he is abandoned, put out of his continuum of correct experience, nothing is acceptable, and nothing accepted. Want is all there is, there is nothing to use, to grow on, to fulfill his requirement for experience, for the experiences must be the expected ones and nothing in his evolving ancestors' experience has prepared him to be left alone, asleep or awake, and even less to be left alone to cry.

Jean Liedloff, *The Continuum Concept*
In Search of Happiness Lost

Anthropologist Jean Liedloff believes that the Yequana Indians, living deep in the jungles of Venezuela, are the happiest people on earth.

And as we read about them, it doesn't take much to be convinced.

What Jean Liedloff describes leads inevitably to questions about whether it is possible to apply the way of life of this tribal people to ourselves amidst the intense pressures of our modern way of life.

In relation to the Yequana, we need to ask ourselves:
- What creates their confidence, their sense of self, their spontaneity, their joy and their total lack of judgment, criticism, blame or competitiveness?

- How do they develop their ability to know what they want – whether comfort, reassurance, adventure, friendship or joy – and to have their needs met free of shame?

- What in their culture gives them the confidence to make their own decisions, and to accept each other's decisions free of any need to judge, persuade, cajole, convince or manipulate others to another way of thinking?

- Where do they find the strength and energy to carry heavy burdens long distances, even though their small musculature doesn't compare to a western man's? And in contrast, why do strong western men get tired with a lighter load at shorter distances?

- Where do they find their joy and constant sense of humor, even in the middle of the night when they suddenly wake everybody up to share a joke?

Thinking about the Yequana, we can extract nine Yequana principles that lead to a joy-filled heart. These principles are available to anyone, whether we live in the jungles of Venezuela or the jungle of our modern lifestyle and environment.

Living with a joy-filled heart as the Yequana do involves resonating with these nine principles and putting them into action in our life. Each time we apply them in action, we raise our level of joy and our potential to live permanently from a joy-filled heart.

PRINCIPLE #1: ENJOY THE JOURNEY AND LAUGH

In her book, *The Coherence Continuum*, Jean Liedloff describes a fundamental difference between the western explorers in the Venezuelan jungle and the Yequana Indians who were guiding them.

Days before the arduous journey up river, the westerners – two Italians and Jean from the USA – were dreading the obstacles they would meet on the way. And their expectations were fully realized: dragging the canoe upstream, carrying it past waterfalls, wading through water trying to direct the canoe through rocky areas in the river; cutting their shins; often standing in the water pinned between the canoe and the rocks – all to the accompaniment of swearing, upset, anger, frustration and exhaustion.

Meanwhile the Yequana who accompanied them and faced the same obstacles were joking and laughing. When one of them was pinned against the rocks and cut by jagged surfaces they all laughed, and the one pinned against the rock laughed the loudest. And for them, each success in maneuvering the canoe was a victory they all celebrated.

Jean Liedloff describes how this enjoyment, laughter and joking was a way of life for the Yequana. Sometimes in the middle of the night one of them would wake up and tell a joke. The others, fast asleep and snoring, would instantly wake up, laugh at the joke and then within seconds fall back to sleep once more – undisturbed by being woken up, and free of any judgment that sleep is better than waking up to enjoy a laugh.

Sometimes while walking across a narrow log over a stream, a Yequana would turn during this delicate balancing act to tell a joke to the friends following behind him. They would all laugh and then once more the man would continue across the log.

The Yequana do whatever they do with laughter and jokes. They don't waste their energy in tension or upset, or wishing that what they are experiencing or doing should be different from the way it is.

So Yequana Principle #1 says: laugh, joke and enjoy the journey – no matter what is happening. Laugh in the face of obstacles, laugh for joy, laugh with your friends at every opportunity. Their message to us is to enjoy everything to the full, exactly as it is, without wasting energy on complaints or being negative about the situation we are in.

Complaining about the way something is, is a way of life for most of us in the West, in the same way that laughter and acceptance is a way of life for the Yequana.

Creating new neural pathways for seeing the humor in all the events of our life is a new possibility we have the choice to resonate with.

If doing the Repatterning, return to {B a} p.247

⌢

PRINCIPLE #2: PEACE OF MIND

Jean Liedloff noticed that when strangers entered a Yequana village, they would immediately go and sit in the shade under the round roof in the center of the clearing.

They sat in silence for an hour and a half, not talking to each other or to anyone in the village.

Finally a woman from the village would place a little food on the ground in front of them. After a while the strangers would eat in silence.

Later a villager would approach, leaning on one of the poles. Softly he would speak a few words. After a few minutes one of the strangers would gently respond, also with a few words. Always silence enveloped them between their words.

One by one other villagers would join the group, the exchanges gradually becoming more lively. No one interrupted anyone. Their voices were free of all emotional tension. Each person maintained their serenity. Soon they were all laughing and eating together – their peace of mind intact.

After a villager returns from a long trading trip, he follows the same steps: stillness, silence and re-integration into family and village life with a sense of peace for all.

Jean Liedloff observes that in our western societies we express ourselves through compensating behaviors. These behaviors vary, she said, according to the deprivation we experienced in our infancy, when we missed the first eight months of twenty-four hour contact with our mother – known as the in-arms phase of development.

The Yequana aren't deprived of touch contact with their mother during the first eight months of life and consequently all the baby's needs are met during this most important developmental phase.

Right from birth the Yequana know what it is to be serene, to have peace of mind. And they place a priority on maintaining this inner peace in any situation that might otherwise disturb their peace of mind.

Even when bartering, the Yequana trust in an innate sense of fairness both in themselves and the person they are trading with. For them, maintaining their peace of mind and good relations are more important than winning the best bargain.

For most of us in the west, we live with distraction, stress, competition, win-lose, and a lack of peace.

For many of us, creating new neural pathways for living peacefully – with ourselves, family members, friends and colleagues at work – would involve a 180 degree turn-around. And making peace a priority before our need to have our own way, to be right, to win, could be life-changing. Even world-changing!

If doing the Repatterning, return to {C a} p.248

～

PRINCIPLE #3: WORK IS PLAY

The Yequana don't have a word in their vocabulary for work – only a Spanish derivative for this word.

It is taken for granted that everyone wants to stay active. And they don't differentiate between work and play. Tasks that are completed with laughter and joking are viewed as play.

The Yequana only do a task as long as they enjoy doing it. If work becomes tedious, they either do something else or they find a way to have fun while doing it. If involved in something monotonous, they find creative ways to do the work so as to make it interesting.

For example, they often join together as a group to do a monotonous task like putting up a roof. They make a grand party out of the event. Or the women, who need to walk down the mountainside three times a day to fetch water, do so with other women and their babies. On each of the three long trips, the women talk and joke as they go and then lie in the water with each other and their babies.

The Yequana don't work out of obligation or force, but because they want to – because it brings them pleasure. They are also free of judgment about someone who doesn't want to work because it doesn't bring them pleasure.

Jean Liedloff describes how Cesar, a Tauripan Indian, who had lived in a Venezuelan city, returned to the jungle and decided once more to live as a Tauripan.

For five years he and his Tauripan wife lived with his Yequana friend Pepe and Pepe's family.

As Cesar didn't like to work, he didn't create his own garden or help Pepe in his garden. Pepe provided Cesar's family with produce, and Pepe's sons, who loved to fish, provided both families with what they needed. Everyone was happy.

After five years Cesar decided he wanted a garden and Pepe helped him fell the trees and prepare the space. The two men enjoyed working together, laughing and joking.

No one pressured Cesar to work. When Cesar was ready, then he too like Pepe and his sons, free of pressure and judgments, was able to re-discover his innate desire to be active and work with pleasure.

In the west, this attitude is most often found amongst athletes, entrepreneurs and artists who have a vision of what they want to achieve and how they want to live. They do what it takes to reach their vision with pleasure, even if money is not forthcoming.

Others may love their work, but for too many reaching the top involves long hours, competition, obligations to earn more money than is actually needed, loss of time with families, exhaustion, illness, and for some a premature death.

Re-discovering joy in work and work as play may be one of the most significant changes for the future of our modern world.

If doing the Repatterning, return to {D a} p.248

⁓

PRINCIPLE #4: FREEDOM FROM BLAME AND PUNISHMENT

One of the extraordinary qualities of the Yequana Indians in the Venezuelan jungle is that they don't blame anyone for anything. They trust that others don't want to hurt them, and if they do hurt them it is understood to be an accident – the equivalent of accidentally being hit by the branch of a tree.

One day a nine-year old came to Jean Liedloff for help. He had a serious wound in his abdomen. When she asked him what had caused it, he calmly responded, "An arrow." Jean then asked whose arrow. The boy calmly named his older brother "with about as much emotion as if I had asked him the name of a flower," Jean writes. The child had no sense of blame or upset.

Other boys, along with the older brother, stopped to watch as Jean dressed the wound. There was no guilt about what the older brother had done, or fear of punishment, or grief and anger in the younger child about what had happened. When the child's mother came and was told what had happened she said softly, "Really?" It was simply an accident. Her child was taken care of and she left to continue her daily tasks.

If they need to correct a behavior they do so, but with no sense of criticism of the person, or judgment that they are bad. They simply let the child know what he or she needs to be doing.

If doing the Repatterning, return to {E a} p.250

⁓

PRINCIPLE #5: MAKING YOUR OWN DECISIONS AND HONORING OTHERS' DECISIONS

The Yequana Indians of the Venezuelan jungle make their own decisions and honor the decisions of others, free of any need to influence, cajole, persuade, coerce or manipulate others to think and decide otherwise. They don't pressure each other and they don't impose their will on each other.

They are **interested** in each other's decisions, but free of any need to impose their own desire.

They believe each person is capable of making a decision, and if someone makes a decision it means they have the ability to do so. Small children naturally look to their elders for decision-making, but even quite young children take responsibility for their own decisions.

Once, preparing to go on an expedition, Jean asked Anchu, the chief, whether Tadehah – a ten year old boy – could come along with them. Tadehah said he wanted to go, and with some other Yequana villagers they started up the river.

After a week there was a disagreement and the Yequana men decided to go home. As they were leaving, they turned to Tadehah and said, "Come along!" Tadehah gently said "No" and the men, accepting his decision, continued on their way. The child had decided what was right for him and there was no thought of dissuading him, even though they were leaving him alone with three foreigners.

If doing the Repatterning, return to {F a} p.251

❧

PRINCIPLE #6: FINDING YOUR OWN PACE AND HONORING ANOTHER'S PACE

Jean Liedloff learned an important lesson about finding her own pace through Anchu, the chief of the village where she stayed.

She had just exchanged a glass ornament for seven large canes of sugar. Anchu and another Indian carried six of the cane stalks on their shoulders and Anchu left the seventh on the ground for Jean to carry, which did not make her happy.

The journey back was an arduous one through the jungles and up two mountains to the village, which was located on top of a third mountain.

But Jean accepted that Anchu did nothing by accident and tended to use opportunities to guide her in the ways of the Yequana. So she lifted the cane on her shoulder.

Anchu waited for Jean to lead the way. Very soon Jean discovered that the strain she was expecting fell away. She found her own comfortable pace and Anchu and the other villager fell in with her pace.

When on expeditions with western men, Jean felt she had to keep up with them: she needed to prove herself, she grit her teeth and pushed herself to compete with the men. And she always felt she was being negatively judged by them.

With the Yequana on the other hand, she enjoyed her own pace, simply walking through the jungle with a sugar cane on her shoulder, feeling the strength of her body and enjoying being in partnership with the Indians.

She experienced the joy of pooling their energy as they walked, and most important she realized that for the Yequana, time on the path and the arrival were equally enjoyable. They didn't mind slowing down to her pace and she didn't need to push herself to stay up with their pace. They all enjoyed their time on the path together.

With this new understanding she began to see the possible secret of why the Yequana and Tauripan Indians were able to carry heavier burdens for longer distances than the more muscular white men: they do what they do without wasting their energy with tension of any kind. They know the pace to move at.

If doing the Repatterning, return to {G a} p.252

PRINCIPLE #7: FREEDOM FROM COMPETITION

Jean Leidloff was amazed that during all the time she spent with the Yequana Indians she never saw the children fight or argue with each other, and she never observed any competition amongst them.

The Yequana have no competitive games or championships, only a series of matches in which all of them do their best to achieve excellence, but no one needs to be the best.

The Yequana are motivated by their desire to be **their** best, not by a desire to beat others and be **the** best.

Similarly Jean never observed sibling rivalry or jealousy. She never saw Yequana children hitting each other – except one case of a little boy who had lived in a Venezuelan city.

Each Yequana infant is given twenty-four hour physical contact with the mother during the first eight months after birth. After about eight months, when the infant is ready to start crawling and exploring the world, the infant initiates its own separation from the mother.

As a result, a new baby is simply taking the place with the mother that the older child has voluntarily left. So there is no rivalry. There is nothing to be jealous about. The mother is available to all her children if and when and how they need her.

In contrast, in the Western world where the baby has missed this twenty-four-hour-a-day in-arms phase, the child and later the adult is unconsciously left wanting what he or she never had.

In the Western world, when a new baby appears to be having what was missing for the older sibling, the younger sibling becomes an object of jealousy. Sibling quarrels, competition, bad temper, hitting and unresolved tensions throughout childhood – and into adulthood too – are the result.

If doing the Repatterning, return to {H a} p.253

⟳

PRINCIPLE #8: THE MOTHER-CHILD BOND

From the moment a Yequana baby is born, it is in physical contact with its mother.

For about eight months the baby is part of its mother's busy life: carried on her back or on a hip, he or she is taken everywhere with the mother.

The baby suckles whenever the impulse arises. He moves as she moves – bending, straightening, kneeling. He even stays with her during the vigorous stomping dance at nightfall – his head bouncing up and down while he continues to sleep peacefully.

At night the baby stays with the mother – skin to skin contact. He is fully a part of her world. When he wants excitement he signals it with bouncing up and down and gurgling in response to the kissing and teasing of others.

Liedloff describes how the infant in its mother's arms is in a state of rightness – of peace and feeling welcomed. For millions of years babies are held by their mothers after their birth as a way of providing the immediate need for imprinting by the mother and baby – which takes precedence over a mother's tiredness or hunger.

This bonding imprint must be completed immediately. The in-arms stage for the baby – up to about the first eight months – is when he receives whatever he needs without doing anything.

As a result of completing this in-arms stage, Yequana babies are happy and relaxed. The Yequana baby rarely cries. If it does, just a small noise is enough to signal its need. As the mother immediately responds to her baby's signals, Yequana babies never scream. The Yequana mother would never dream of letting her baby cry without responding to its need.

The baby is at peace with himself. His infancy of living as an integrated part of his mother's life from the safety and security of his contact with her is the foundation for an enriched life. His mind is flooded with sensations, variety and activity as he moves through his mother's day – accompanying her down the mountainside to collect water and while she completes all her daily routines.

As his energy is mobilized through her activities, any excess energy on the part of the infant is naturally discharged through the mother's movements. As a result he remains relaxed, soft, contented and happy.

In contrast, western babies for the most part are separated from the mother at birth in numerous ways:

- weighing and washing take precedence over the initial and immediate imprinting between the mother and baby. This missed bonding imprint continues to be the most important loss for the infant and the mother.

- The baby is usually removed from his place of safety in his mother's arms – moving with her, smelling her, seeing her, touching her, hearing her voice and heartbeat and suckling when he needs to. Instead he is placed in a crib that is still and inanimate.

- Instead of staying connected to her, he is in a hospital ward surrounded by other wailing babies who are also suffering from the afterbirth shock of their first separation in nine months from their mother's womb.

- In the baby's first eight months after the birth, being held in the mother's arms is all too rare: he sleeps alone; he is placed in a crib or pram; instead of being a part of the mother's life and world, he more often than not is lying down with only a few hanging toys to play with. Instead of contact with her, he is given a blankie or teddy bear and a pacifier as a substitute for the mother he yearns and cries for. Instead of being fed when he needs to, he is often put on scheduled feeding. Instead of his cry being understood as a signal for some need to be met, it is often ignored and he is allowed to cry himself to sleep or exhaustion. Instead of constant movement even while he sleeps in the day, he has stillness.

- He rarely has skin-to-skin contact with his mother. Once a Resonance Repatterning practitioner shared that her baby was screaming and no matter what she did, he wouldn't stop. Finally in a moment of desperation and instinctual knowing, she removed his clothes and her own top and held him skin to skin. Instantly he stopped crying.

- Because babies are deprived of the eight months in-arms phase, they are driven to discharge their constricted energy – caused by the separation and the lack of natural movement when carried by the mother. They try to discharge this energy by stiffening their body, arching their back, wriggling, waving their arms, thumb sucking and screaming. They are often difficult to hold when picked up.

- When the infant is only held by someone who is sitting quietly, it conditions the baby to think of life as still, dull and slow.

If doing the Repatterning, return to {I a} p.254

PRINCIPLE # 9: INITIATING SEPARATION

For the Yequana, the infant initiates its own separation from the mother.

When the infant is ready, he begins to crawl on his belly and then on hands and knees.

The baby explores its world with all the confidence, trust and self-reliance that have been developed through the in-arms phase. The infant knows he is able to return to the mother whenever he needs to: whether out of a need, for reassurance or simply to make sure she is available.

The baby's self-confidence is determined by her availability.

The mother is busy but relaxed. She is present and calm. She gives her baby attention when he comes to her, free of any sense of inconvenience or that her time is being wasted. She gives her baby what he needs without giving over-attention or being possessive (which is not giving love, but trying to **get** love from the baby).

As the baby trusts that the mother is available for food, reassurance or help, he returns to her less often and spends more time playing and actively seeking out other children and things to play with that expand his capacities and learning.

If doing the Repatterning, return to {J a} p.256

The two deprivations

As we can see from reading the nine Yequana principles, most of us have been deprived, to one extent or another, of (1) the after-birth imprinting along with the eight months in-arms phase, (2) initiating our own separation from our mother and (3) the freedom to explore our world safely, with our mother being available if we need her.

Any issue in our life has a relationship to these three deprivations. Transforming what we resonate with in terms of these deprivations and beginning to integrate one or more of the nine Yequana Principles leads to a joy-filled heart.

FURTHER READING

Jean Liedloff. *The Coherence Continuum.*

8. THE JOY-FILLED HEART REPATTERNING

A. Identify the present problem
Ask, "What problem are you facing in your life at this time?" *[cr] *(will be on/umb on).*

B. (mcs) Principle #1 is needed? – Laughter at every opportunity and acceptance of what is
Do {a–c} in sequence.

a. Read Principle #1 *p.234*
Ask, "What did you learn from this principle?" *[cr] with "I (*name the learning in a positive statement – leave out 'learn'*) (will be off/umb off for the higher learning).*

b. (mcs) We need to know the non-coherence involved with the loss of laughter and acceptance of what is?
Ask, "What situation do you have trouble accepting – where you lose your ability to respond to the situation with laughter?" *[cr] with "When (*name the situation),* I accept it as it is, free of complaints and upset, and I lighten up and laugh" *(will be off/umb off).*

c. Identify the coherence you need in relation to laughter and acceptance of what is.
(mcs) {1–8}. *[cr] *(will be off/umb off).*

1. I accept challenging situations with a sense of humor and a sense of fun.
2. I release tension through laughter.
3. I enjoy laughing with others.
4. I find excuses to enjoy laughter, joking, and having fun when with others.
5. I choose to laugh in situations where I would usually complain or feel upset.
6. I enjoy harmless teasing that makes everyone laugh.

7. Even when there's nothing to laugh about, I let go of my tension and find something humorous that makes me laugh.
8. I celebrate with joy and laughter.

C. (mcs) Principle #2 is needed? – Peace of mind

Do {a–c} in sequence.

a. Read Principle #2 *p.236*
Ask, "What did you learn from this principle?" *[cr] with "I (*name the learning in a positive statement – leave out 'learn'*) (will be off/umb off*).

b. (mcs) We need to know the non-coherence involved with a loss of peace of mind?
Ask, "In what situation do you lose your peace of mind?" *[cr] with "When (*name the situation*) I settle into stillness and silence and regain my peace of mind before I talk or go into action" *(will be off/umb off*).

c. Identify the coherence you need in relation to peace of mind.
(mcs) {1–6 }. *[cr] *(will be off/umb off*).
1. I settle into my peace of mind when I am with others, allowing myself to be quiet and still.
2. I allow others time to settle into their peace of mind.
3. I take my time to settle and center myself when facing a challenge or feeling upset.
4. I maintain or regain my peace of mind during my daily activities by taking time out for stillness, silence and slowing down.
5. I accept (silence • challenges) as an opportunity to connect to my peace of mind once more.
6. During a charged situation, I allow the conversation to move at a pace that supports peacefulness and a relaxed sense of connection.

D. (mcs) Principle #3 is needed? – Do work or tasks you enjoy and create enjoyment from work

Do {a–c} in sequence.

a. Read Principle #3 *p.237*

Ask, "What did you learn from this principle?" *[cr] with "I (*name the learning in a positive statement – leave out 'learn'*) (*will be off/umb off*).

b. **(mcs) We need to know the non-coherence involved with the lack of pleasure in doing a particular task?**
   (mcs) {1–2}.

   1. **Doing work you do not enjoy:** *Ask,* "What tasks or work do you **not** enjoy doing?" *[cr] with "When I (*name the task you don't enjoy doing*), I discover creative ways to make it fun and interesting, and if I still dislike it I do something else" (*will be off/umb off*).

   2. **Resentment or anxiety about someone else not working:** *Ask,* "In what situation do you get resentful or anxious because others are not working or helping as you would like them to?" *[cr] with "When (*name the situation where the client is resentful or anxious*), I relax, keep doing what I love to do, and trust that (*name person*) will discover what he/she loves to do in time" (*will be off/umb off*).

c. **Identify the coherence you need in relation to doing tasks that bring you pleasure and allowing others to discover the tasks that bring them pleasure**
   (mcs) {1–12}. *[cr] (*will be off/umb off*).

   1. When I am doing something that is tedious, I take a rest from doing it and find something else to do that brings me pleasure.
   2. I only do a task if I enjoy doing it or if I discover how to do it with creativity and pleasure.
   3. I give myself the time to discover what job gives me pleasure, free of guilt and self-blame.
   4. I do what gives me pleasure without judging others for not helping me, if helping doesn't give them pleasure.
   5. If no one wants to do a task because it feels tedious, we explore ways of doing it together in a way that brings pleasure and fun to all of us.
   6. I trust the innate pleasure each of us has from working, and in supporting the mutual needs of the group.

7. I am free of resentment when others don't help/work and I am happy that I love what I do and am energized by what I do.
8. I share the fruits of my work with others, whether they help me/work or not.
9. I do those things that make my heart sing.
10. I rediscover my readiness to find pleasure in each thing I do and accomplish.
11. I give people the space to discover what makes their heart sing.
12. I enjoy and celebrate each thing I do and (I stop focusing on • complaining about) what I have not completed or done.

E. (mcs) Principle #4 is needed? – Freedom from blame and punishment

Do {a–c} in sequence.

a. Read Principle #4 *p.239*
Ask, "What did you learn from this principle?" *[cr] with "I (*name the learning in a positive statement – leave out 'learn'*) (will be off/umb off).*

b. (mcs) We need to know the non-coherence involved with blame?
(mcs) {1–3} for the one involved.

1. **(mcs) Blame of someone else is involved?**
Ask, "Who do you blame for doing something that has hurt or upset you – what do you blame this person for?" *[cr] with "I accept that (*name person*) made the mistake of (*name what you blame him/her for*) and I regain my peace of mind" *(will be off/umb off).*

2. **(mcs) Blame of self is involved?**
Ask, "What do you blame yourself for?" *[cr] with "I accept that I made the mistake of (*name what you blame yourself for*) and I regain my peace of mind" *[cr] (will be off/umb off).*

3. **(mcs) Being blamed by someone else is involved?**
Ask, "What have you been blamed for?" *[cr] with "I accept that (*name person*) made the mistake of blaming me for (*name what he/she blames you for*) and I regain my peace of mind" *(will be off/umb off).*

c. **Identify the coherence needed in relation to freedom from blame.** (**mcs**) {1–6}. *[**cr**] *(will be off/umb off)*.

   1. I see the best in others.
   2. I accept that each person manifests their inner pain and deprivation in ways that can hurt themselves and others.
   3. When I hurt (*name person*) I know that in my core I am free of all desire to hurt him/her. I do my best to correct the situation.
   4. I maintain my peace of mind both when I am hurt by another or when I hurt another.
   5. I accept myself and am lovable even though I hurt (*name person*) • I accept (*name person*) as lovable, even though he/she made the mistake of (*name the hurt in {E b 3}*).
   6. *Ask,* "What actions do you want to do in relation to being free of blame, criticism and punishment?"

F. **(mcs) Principle #5 is needed? – Make your own decisions and honor others' decisions**
   Do {a–c} in sequence.

   a. **Read Principle #5** *p.240*
      Ask, "What did you learn from this principle?" *[**cr**] with "I (*name the learning in a positive statement – leave out 'learn'*) *(will be off/umb off)*.

   b. **(mcs) We need to know the non-coherence involved with decision-making?**
      (**mcs**) {1–2} for the one needed.

      1. **(mcs) Making your own decisions is involved?**
         Ask, "What decision do you need to make (*possibly concerning the problem in {A}*)?" *[**cr**] with "(I trust my ability to make a wise decision that serves me well and allows me to resolve (*name the problem*) • I make my own decisions and accept the consequences with poise)" *(will be off/umb off)*.

2. (**mcs**) **Dealing with another's decision is involved?**
    Ask, "Are you dealing with someone whose decision you don't agree
    with?" *[**cr**] with "I allow (*name person*) to be responsible for his/her
    own decision and trust in his/her capacity to do so and to accept the
    consequences" *(will be off/umb off).*

c. **Identify the coherence you need in relation to decisions**
    (**mcs**) {1–9}. *[**cr**] *(will be off/umb off).*
    1. I make decisions that bring me joy.
    2. I provide (*name person*) with options and accept the option he/she
        chooses or doesn't choose.
    3. I listen to others' opinions free of being (persuaded to change my
        mind • cajoled into their way of thinking • manipulated).
    4. I support (*name person*) in making decisions that bring him/her joy.
    5. I recognize that there are consequences to every decision and I accept
        the consequences free of self-blame and negative judgments.
    6. I understand that (*name person*) faces the consequences of his/
        her decisions and I am free of negative judgments about his/her
        decisions.
    7. I feel strong, confident and self-reliant making decisions based on
        what is both practical and what makes my heart sing.
    8. I give (*name person*) the freedom to make decisions appropriate to
        his/her age and development so he/she becomes strong, confident
        and self-reliant.
    9. I have the capacity to choose what is best for me.

G. (**mcs**) **Principle #6 is needed? – Find your own pace and honor another's pace**
Do {a–c} in sequence.
a. **Read Principle #6** *p.240*
    Ask, "What did you learn from this principle?" *[**cr**] with "I (*name the
    learning in a positive statement – leave out 'learn'*) *(will be off/umb off).*

b. **(mcs) We need to know the non-coherence involved with finding your own pace?**
Ask, "Where do you feel hurried or pressured? What negative judgment are you afraid of?"
*[cr] with "I let go of my fear that I will be judged for (*name the negative judgment*) and I find the pace that energizes me and brings me joy" *(will be off/umb off)*.

c. **Identify the coherence you need in relation to finding your own pace (mcs) {1–7 }.** *[cr] *(will be off/umb off)*.
   1. I find my own pace and am totally energized by what I am doing.
   2. I let go of the pressure (I impose on myself • I feel others impose on me • (*name person*) imposes on me) that makes me tense.
   3. I respect each person's own pacing and I slow my pace to accommodate his/her need to go slower.
   4. (*Name person*) happily slows down his/her/their pace to accommodate my need to go slower.
   5. (I have all the time I need to complete (*name where you feel hurried or what you feel pressured to do*) • I enjoy the journey as much as the arrival).
   6. (I avoid wasting my energy on tension, complaints and feeling pressured • Everything gets done in the right time and at the right pace).
   7. I enjoy doing what I do at my own pace.

H. (mcs) Principle #7 is needed? – Freedom from competition
Do {a–c} in sequence.

a. **Read Principle #7** *p.242*
Ask, "What did you learn from this principle?" *[cr] with "I (*name the learning in a positive statement – leave out 'learn'*) (will be off/umb off)*.

b. **(mcs) We need to know the non-coherence involved with competition?**
Ask, "In what situation do you find yourself competing to be better than others, or you feel jealous of someone's success or inadequate in relation

to someone's success?" *[**cr**] with "I enjoy achieving excellence and being the best I am capable of and I enjoy that (*name person/others*) achieves excellence and does the best he/she is capable of (*will be off/umb off*).

c. **(mcs) Identify the coherence you need in relation to freedom from competition**
(**mcs**) {1–7}. *[**cr**] (*will be off/umb off*).

1. I resolve the mother-infant bond that I missed with my mother during the in arms phase, and enjoy (*name person/others*) receiving the love and attention he/she needs.
2. I let go of my need to win and be better than (*name person*) and I maintain my peace of mind.
3. I enjoy (*name person*) achieving his/her own personal best and I am free of jealousy, rivalry, tension, loss of confidence or any sense of inadequacy.
4. (*Name person*) enjoys me achieving my own personal best and is free of jealousy, rivalry, tension, loss of confidence or any sense of inadequacy on his/her part.
5. (I understand that when I am competing for someone's attention, I have activated my own deprived infant aspect, whose need for total bonding was not met • I stop judging myself and (*name person*) and resolve my own bonding-separation issues).
6. (I let go of feeling jealous of (*name person*)'s success and feeling inadequate • I resolve my bonding and separation issues and get on with achieving my own personal best).
7. I give genuine credit and appreciation for what (*name person*) has achieved.

I. **(mcs) Principle #8 is needed? – The mother-child bond for a joy-filled life**
Do {a–c} in sequence.
a. **Read some or all of Principle #8** *p.243*
Ask, "What did you learn from this principle?" *[**cr**] with "I (*name the learning in a positive statement – leave out 'learn'*) (*will be off/umb off*).

b. **(mcs) We need to know the non-coherence involved with the mother-child bond?**

Ask, "What was your after birth bonding experience with your mother? Were you separated from her?" *[cr] with "In spite of (*name the separation*), I trust that (the experience of bonding with my mother can be supplied at any age • I regain my sense of rightness, being welcomed and having the comfort of bonded love • I have bonded love with my intimate partner)" *(will be off/umb off).*

c. **Identify the coherence you need in relation to the mother-child bond (mcs) {1–21}.** *[cr] *(will be off/umb off).*
   1. All my needs are met without my having to do anything.
   2. Life is exciting, active and safe.
   3. I feel right from deep within myself.
   4. I am supported in having my need for love met.
   5. I am seen and loved.
   6. I feel safe and secure.
   7. Love is accessible at every moment.
   8. I am a part of life.
   9. I am fed on all levels.
   10. I am connected to the heart-beat of love.
   11. I experience the energy of love through skin to skin contact.
   12. I am at peace, totally relaxed, soft and trusting.
   13. I am connected to love.
   14. I am held with love and I hold with love.
   15. Love pours through my eyes and connects me to each person I meet.
   16. I open my heart to each person I meet and receive their love.
   17. My heart attracts love from within others and opens their heart.
   18. I am strong and confident, open to new learning and ready to handle what life brings.
   19. Love and connection help me discharge excess energy from building up so I stay relaxed and open to life.
   20. When I cry for help it is my signal that something needs to be set right and my mother sets it right calmly and free of fuss.

21. I receive all the touch and affection I need for a loving bond, and take this into my partnerships so I experience bonding as affection distinct from sexual bonding

J. **(mcs) Principle #9 is needed? – Initiate your own separation from the mother for a joy-filled life**
Do {a–d} in sequence.

a. **Read Principle #9** *p.245*
Ask, "What did you learn from this principle?" *[cr] with "I (*name the learning in a positive statement – leave out 'learn'*) (will be off/umb off).*

b. **(mcs) We need to know the non-coherence involved with separating from your mother?**
Explain: As an infant you didn't choose to separate from your mother.
Ask, "Do you have any memory when you were forced to separate from your mother?"

Ask, "What do you want instead of that experience?" *[cr] with "Instead of (*name the past experience of enforced separation*), (*name what you want instead*)" (will be off/umb off).*

c. **(mcs) We need to identify the freedom to explore your world?**
Ask, "Do you have any memory of being constrained, not given the freedom to explore in the way you wanted to?" *[cr] with "Instead of (*name the experience of constraint / not being free to explore as you wanted*), I explore my world, connect with others and learn, and also know that my mother is available whenever I need her" (will be off/ umb off).*

d. **Identify the coherence you need in relation to separation from your mother.**
(mcs) {1–12 }. *[cr] (will be off/umb off).*
1. I am ready to explore my world, free of needing my mother's full attention.

2. My mother is available when I need her.
3. My mother is relaxed and calm and provides me with what I need and then I happily return to exploring my world.
4. I seek out other people of all age groups who connect with me, support me and give me a wide variety of positive experiences.
5. I bring pleasure to all the people I meet as I explore my world.
6. My capacities grow as I explore my world and my mother gives me unconditional acceptance and love.
7. My father shows by example what is expected of me and how to be my best in the world.
8. My mother expects me to be safe, to be instinctively in touch with what supports my survival, and to reconnect to her whenever I need her.
9. As I grow I express my new-found abilities and energy through joyful work, intimate partnership and friendships.
10. I trust that my mother is available when I need her attention and as a result my self-confidence and self-reliance grow.
11. When I need help I ask for it.
12. I know how to look after myself and my mother supports me by her presence.

K. Identify the point of choice for new possibilities

Do {a–f} in sequence.

a. (mcs) Read the following

When we are deprived of the in arms phase with our mother, we most likely experience any of the following states: loneliness, abandonment, pain, anger, fear, unworthiness and/or grief.

Our in-born expectation that our bonding and growing needs will be met without our needing to do anything was not met. As a consequence the need for a positive in-arms experience still remains. The deprivation we feel doesn't diminish with time. Whatever pain we originally experienced keeps repeating itself in our life. Bonding deprivation is reflected in our intimate relationships or lack of relationship. For example:

- the pattern of a woman who is abandoned by the men she loves and is left weeping and angry

- a man who is addicted to short-term romantic relationships but never finds what he is looking for

- people suffering from illness, drugs, alcohol or eating disorders

Our pain from the missing bonding-separation of the first few years of life always manifests as non-coherent compensations.

It is as though we keep limiting our choices to the non-coherent infant response for the missing in arms stage when needs were not met. Once we become conscious of our non-coherent infant pattern and change our resonance with it, we are able to access a broader range of choices and decisions.

There are limitless possibilities in the infinite field of energy. We have the choice to create new intentions for who we want to be and how we want to relate and what we want to achieve in our life. When we resonate with the positive, we attract the positive from the limitless field of energy.

b. **Identify the point of choice**
   Ask, "Thinking about the Yequana and what they represent for you, what do you want to have in your relationships/life? What do you want to be, achieve or contribute in your life?" *[**cr**] with "I want, choose and am ready to (*name what you want to have, achieve or contribute*) (*will be off/ umb off*).

c. **Need it fulfills**
   Ask, "What need would having, achieving (*name {b}*) fulfill for you?" *[**cr**] with "I (*name the need*)" (*will be off/umb off*).

d. **Positive feeling**
   Ask, "How would you feel when this need is realized?" *[**cr**] with "I (*name the feeling*)" (*will be off/umb off*).

L. Identify the Energizing Options for a joy-filled life
Do {a–c} in sequence.
a. (mcs) Client needs to wear the CYW Lenses?
(**mcs**) for which color lens is needed for each eye.

b. (**mcs**) An energy contact is needed? (**mcs**) An (acupuncture point/ jin shin point) is needed? *See* SPIRAL UP! *for Jin Shin points and p.127 for some Acupuncture point options.* (**mcs**) The CYW Torch/Tuning Forks is needed on the point? (**mcs**) for details. **Do the energy contact while talking through the visualization.**

c. The visualization: *Say,* "Close your eyes. Relax and slow your breathing down. I will talk you through the following visualization to create new neural pathways in your body-brain for limitless possibilities.

After practitioner is clear on what client needs to see and feel as listed below, practitioner reads the following visualization slowly and with pauses:

• See what you most want (*practitioner names it for client {K b, c}*).

• Feel (*name the client's positive feeling {K d}*).

• See yourself lovingly held by your ideal mother from the moment of your birth and for at least eight months – carried on her back or hip, enjoying the variety of life through her movements and daily activities.

• Feel the safety and security of being in contact with her – your ideal mother.

• Feel the excitement of life as you share her busy life from where she holds you on her hip or her back.

• Hear her heart beat at night when you sleep with her, held close, feeding whenever you need to.

- Experience all your needs being met effortlessly.

- After you have received all that you need, without having to do anything except express your happiness, contentment and peace of mind, feel your natural impulse to separate from your mother. It is your choice. You are ready to start moving out to explore your world separate from your mother, but always seeing that she is present in your life.

- See yourself returning to your mother whenever you want so you know she is available for you whenever you need her.

- See yourself needing to return to your mother less and less often as you enjoy exploring and learning, gaining confidence and self-reliance, and playing and learning from others – younger and older as well as children of your own age.

- Trust that you can return to your ideal mother for reassurance, love, acceptance and help whenever you need her.

- Feel how you are free to discharge your own excess energy through your activities and movements – crawling, bouncing, playing, dancing, swinging, running, working at what you love to do.

- You are sure of yourself; you are accustomed to well-being and you bring this well-being to every part of your life. Happiness is the normal condition of being alive and you bring happiness to your life, your play, your work and your relationships. You know joy. You live with joy

- When you are ready, slowly open your eyes and look around with new eyes

M. Positive Action

As you go about your daily tasks, imagine yourself as a baby having what you most wanted in the in arms phase with your mother.

Imagine yourself, when the time comes, initiating your own separation from your mother, full of confidence that you can explore your world and that she is still available at all times for you.

Identify one Yequana Principle that you want to put into practice {1–9}. Begin integrating this principle into your life and enjoy bringing the Yequana way of life into your life in whatever way you want.

HOW TO USE THE JOY-FILLED HEART REPATTERNING IN YOUR DAILY LIFE
EVEN IF YOU HAVE NOT YET ATTENDED A RESONANCE REPATTERNING SEMINAR

- Whenever you have a problem, muscle check or use your felt sense for which Yequana Principle you most need and do an Energizing Option to resonate with it.

- Spend a week focusing on one Yequana Principle, bringing it to your awareness in every part of your life. Actively apply this Principle. Do Energizing Options (or a Resonance Repatterning session) for every issue that arises as you apply this principle.

- Begin to see people you have trouble with as someone who was deprived of coherent bonding and separation. When an infant completes the in arms phase of development they are relaxed, loving, free of tension and all competition to be the best.

RR SESSIONS: If you would like to receive the complete Repatterning with a professional Resonance Repatterning Practitioner, in person or over the phone, go to ResonanceRepatterning.net > Sessions for RR Institute Practitioners worldwide who have listed themselves on the RRI website.

RR SEMINARS: If you would like to attend Resonance Repatterning seminars in person or online, so you can use RR effectively on yourself and/or others, go to ResonanceRepatterning.net > Seminars for the list of teachers endorsed by the Resonance Repatterning Institute to teach.

SPIRAL UP SUPPLIES

The following supplies include those referred to, taught and used in the Resonance Repatterning seminars. Suggestions for how to use each Energizing Option are given in Chloe Wordsworth's book, SPIRAL UP! 127 ENERGIZING OPTIONS TO BE YOUR BEST RIGHT NOW, in her videos and audios demonstrating all the Energizing Options and the Spiral Up Sequences for LIVING IN TUNE.

- The Resonance eStore is committed to Spiral Up Supplies of high quality, each personally endorsed by Chloe Faith Wordsworth and used in Resonance Repatterning seminars and her practice of Resonance Repatterning.

- For the complete list of Spiral Up Supplies available at the Resonance eStore, used in Resonance Repatterning seminars and sessions, go to ResonanceRepatterning.net/estore/

SOUND OPTIONS

God's Cricket Chorus CD

This CD is a one-hour recording of crickets, slowed down to the equivalent of the human lifespan, and sounds like a chorus of ethereal voices, bringing uplift and a sense of awe before nature's beauty and innate harmony.

Resonance Repatterning CD

This moving CD offers an introduction to Resonance Repatterning by the Founder, Chloe Faith Wordsworth, along with teachers, practitioners and clients who share how Resonance Repatterning has reshaped people's lives. You may purchase while the stock lasts or you may listen to it on the Home Page of the ResonanceRepatterning.net website.

Spirit of Love

An inspiring CD with songs like "The Rose" and "You Can Relax Now." Often used in the PRINCIPLES OF RELATIONSHIP and other RR seminars.

Harmonic Overtone Guide

This book and CD by Nestor Kornblum is an example of overtoning at its best. The guide takes you step by step through the process of learning this powerful Energizing Option for yourself. Listening to this master of Harmonic Overtoning on Nestor's CD is a Healing Option in its own right.

Quantum Healing Codes™

Quantum Healing Codes can be purchased on Amazon.

Om Tuning Fork

The Om Tuning Fork, tuned to 136.10 cycles per second, is thought to be a coherent frequency of universal significance for the earth. It can be struck and then held to the left and/or right ears; it can be moved over various body areas, particularly where there is tension, as in headaches; or the stem can be placed on the spine or specific areas of the body. Made in Germany of high quality stainless steel, the Om Tuning Fork is designed specifically for the purpose of vibrational well-being and is beautifully packaged in its own velvet satin-lined pouch.

Tuning Forks for the Complete Scale – C, C#, D, D#, E, F, F#, G, G#, A, A#, B

Made in Germany of high-quality stainless steel and packaged in a beautiful velvet satin-lined pouch, these twelve Tuning Forks make up the complete western scale. They are tuned from the diatonic pitch: A = 220 Hz. As an Energizing Option, you can listen to the vibration or use one or more of the Forks on or over any part of the body, on a Chakra, a Meridian point, a Jin Shin safety energy lock, a reflex point, the spine, etc.

Planetary Tuning Forks

These eleven tuning forks are mathematically tuned to the frequency of the planets, each of which has a particular frequency and is associated with its own characteristic qualities: the Sun, Pluto, Mercury, Mars, Saturn, Jupiter, Earth, Uranus, Moon, Neptune and Venus. Information on how to use planetary intentions, and the signs that may indicate a planetary tuning fork is needed, is provided in SPIRAL UP! 127 ENERGIZING OPTIONS TO BE YOUR BEST RIGHT NOW. *pp.45–50*

Chromatic Tuner

The Chromatic Tuner is used for quickly identifying the note or notes a person needs to tone. Each note (in a one-octave range) is listed on the tuner. When you press the note on the tuner, it gives you the sound you need to tone. The tuner is small and light and can be carried in a purse or pocket for use wherever and whenever you need to 'tune yourself up'.

COLOR AND LIGHT OPTIONS
Flower Pattern Cards

Photographed in India and South Africa, these flowers represent patterns found in sacred geometry. Flowers are said to be the language of the heart. Each flower carries a unique high-frequency note that is not audible to the human ear but is associated with its shape (a manifestation of sacred geometry), its fragrance, texture and its color. The Flower Pattern Cards encourage a shift in perspective as you see light and shadow, color and shape, depth and texture. Focusing on the flower pattern activates the right brain of imagination, feeling, creativity, global vision and receiving a new understanding of your present situation.

Geometric Pattern Cards

Geometric patterns represent the basic patterns or building blocks of the creation. When energy vibrates, the movement creates patterns that are universal – intricate patterns such as spirals and those seen in the movement of water and cloud shapes. Each frequency pattern, experienced as shape, creates coherence in its own unique way. The set of twenty-eight laminated Geometric Pattern Cards consists of six variations of the circle, seven types of spirals, eleven variations of the platonic solids and four crop circle patterns.

ColorYourWorld Lenses

This set of 13 pairs of lenses (and three plastic frames onto which the lenses fit) includes the twelve primary Dinshah colors, plus pink. Each color has a specific frequency and is made from Roscolene gels, as recommended by the Dinshah Health Society. Using the ColorYourWorld Lenses during a Repatterning or as an Energizing Option allows specific color frequencies into the brain-body energy field, often with a dramatic change in perspective, understanding and a sense of well-being. Many people use the CYW Lenses to fine tune their energy or to release stress, tension and depression.

Silk scarves

Nine silk scarves in the colors of the Chakras: red, orange, yellow, green, turquoise, indigo, purple, plus pale pink and white. In gossamer silk, they can be worn around the neck or used in a Resonance Repatterning session when a Chakra or Five Element Acupuncture color is needed.

ColorYourWorld Torch and 13 mini filter gels

The ColorYourWorld Torch comes in a box that includes a silver-mounted natural clear quartz crystal, a mini Mag-Lite with washer cap to hold the crystal and color gels in place, and a set of 13 Roscolene mini gels. The light and color are used to activate and balance the energy field by focusing on specific Jin Shin points, cranial bones, Mu Acupuncture points, Chakras, Meridian points and other body areas.

A book of geometric and Sanskrit gels to use with the CYW Torch is also available.

POSTERS AND LAMINATED GUIDES

- Daily Empowerment Guide

- Inner Cultivation Treasures and Essences

- Chakra Chart

- Five Element qualities

NORTH POLE MAGNET OPTIONS

North Pole Magnets

The **Soother One** is a round two-inch negative north pole magnet disk that penetrates two inches and is used for relieving pain and tension; it can also be used on Acupuncture points, Jin Shin points and the cranial bones.

The **Ceramic Block** negative north pole magnet, 6" x 4" x ½", penetrates six inches and is used for issues involving organs such as the liver, spleen and kidneys. Dr. Philpott, M.D., renowned North Pole Magnet researcher, used the Ceramic Block magnet in cases of cancer and pain involving deeper areas of the body. The **Flex magnet** is the same as the Ceramic Block but is soft and flexible for wrapping round joints or other areas of the body.

The **Magnet Eye Mask** is a powerful way to activate Negative North Pole energy in the retina of the eyes that, along with the pineal gland and intestinal wall, are the only areas in the body that produce melatonin. *Info* VISION

For the above and other Spiral Up Supplies, posters of the Mandala and the Point of Choice poster, and Resonance Repatterning books go to ResonanceRepatterning.net/estore/

ABOUT THE AUTHOR
AND THE RR WEBSITE

Chloe Faith Wordsworth, the founder and developer of Resonance Repatterning®, is the author of QUANTUM CHANGE MADE EASY, SPIRAL UP! 127 ENERGIZING OPTIONS TO BE YOUR BEST RIGHT NOW, the LIVING IN TUNE series and ten Resonance Repatterning manuals. She lives in Arizona and teaches in the USA and abroad.

For more information go to ResonanceRepatterning.net

- To find **a practitioner** and to **advertise yourself as an RR Practitioner**, go to ResonanceRepatterning.net > *SESSIONS TAB*

- For **seminars** go to ResonanceRepatterning.net > *SEMINARS TAB*

- For information on Resonance Repatterning **books and Spiral Up supplies**, go to ResonanceRepatterning.net > *STORE TAB*

- For **Home Study courses** go to ResonanceRepatterning.net > *HOME STUDY TAB*

- To **listen free** to Chloe's LIVING IN TUNE web radio shows, go to ResonanceRepatterning.net > *LIVING IN TUNE TAB*

ACKNOWLEDGMENTS

My thanks to the authors of the quotes at the beginning of each chapter that prepare us for what is to come.

Much appreciation for Rachel Reman, Terry Dobson, Jean Liedloff and Greg Mortenson – the authors of the books whose stories I have shared in LIVING IN TUNE WITH YOUR HEART.

Many thanks to Gail Glanville who in 2008 encouraged me to do the LIVING IN TUNE web radio shows. Without her gentle and consistent push in this direction, I would never have stretched myself to this weekly commitment, and this book would therefore not exist. Thank you, Gail! And Carolyn Winter, thank you for sharing the moving story of your boss that teaches us the power of giving, and for your permission to print it.

Much gratitude to Anthea Guinness for her editing, proof-reading and for the information in her article, "How Green Is Your Fork?", which I used in the Heart Abundance chapter.

Rebecca Hammons' book, *Being Vegetarian*, became an essential part of the ten facts in the Heart Abundance Repatterning. Thank you Rebecca for your inspiration, and a motivation for all of us to make some important choices.

Carol White, thank you for formatting and preparing yet another of my books for publication and being willing to work under pressure. And I continue to be grateful to Leslie Pascoe Chalke for translating this book into Spanish and for so much more. My thanks to Rose Jones for the photo on the front cover.

Constant gratitude to my spiritual teacher and his successor – my ideal of what it is to live from the heart.

Made in the USA
Columbia, SC
03 September 2023

22440227R00150